THE C
PRIVATION

(How to flip ten cents into a dollar)

by Nia Akilah Robinson

FOR AMATEUR PRODUCTION ENQUIRIES

UNITED KINGDOM AND WORLD
EXCLUDING NORTH AMERICA
licensing@concordtheatricals.co.uk
020-7054-7298

Each title is subject to availability from Concord Theatricals, depending upon country of performance.

written permission of the publisher. No one shall share this title, or part of this title, to any social media or file hosting websites.

The moral right of Nia Akilah Robinson to be identified as author of this work has been asserted in accordance with Section 77 of the Copyright, Designs and Patents Act 1988.

USE OF COPYRIGHTED MUSIC

A licence issued by Concord Theatricals to perform this play does not include permission to use the incidental music specified in this publication. In the United Kingdom: Where the place of performance is already licensed by the PERFORMING RIGHT SOCIETY (PRS) a return of the music used must be made to them. If the place of performance is not so licensed then application should be made to PRS for Music (www.prsformusic.com). A separate and additional licence from PHONOGRAPHIC PERFORMANCE LTD (www.ppluk.com) may be needed whenever commercial recordings are used. Outside the United Kingdom: Please contact the appropriate music licensing authority in your territory for the rights to any incidental music.

USE OF COPYRIGHTED THIRD-PARTY MATERIALS

Licensees are solely responsible for obtaining formal written permission from copyright owners to use copyrighted third-party materials (e.g., artworks, logos) in the performance of this play and are strongly cautioned to do so. If no such permission is obtained by the licensee, then the licensee must use only original materials that the licensee owns and controls. Licensees are solely responsible and liable for clearances of all third-party copyrighted materials, and shall indemnify the copyright owners of the play(s) and their licensing agent, Concord Theatricals Ltd., against any costs, expenses, losses and liabilities arising from the use of such copyrighted third-party materials by licensees.

IMPORTANT BILLING AND CREDIT REQUIREMENTS

If you have obtained performance rights to this title, please refer to your licensing agreement for important billing and credit requirements.

NOTE

This programme text was produced from a rehearsal draft of the script, and may differ from the final production.

THE GREAT PRIVATION: HOW TO FLIP TEN CENTS INTO A DOLLAR was first produced by and performed at Theatre503, London, on 14 May 2024. The cast, creative team and production team were as follows:

CHARITY/CHARITY (MODERN DAY) . . . . Christie Fewry
MOTHER/MOTHER (MODERN DAY) . . . . Sydney Sainté
JOHN/JOHN (MODERN DAY) . . . . Jack Gouldbourne
CUFFEE/CUFFEE (MODERN DAY). . . . . Romeo Mika

Writer. . . . . .Nia Akilah Robinson
Director . . . . Kalungi Ssebandeke
Set & Costume Designer. . . . . .Ruth Badila
Lighting Designer . . . . .Chuma Emembolu
Sound Designer . . . . .José Guillermo Puello
Movement Director . . . . Yemurai Zvaraya
Voice and Dialect Coach. . . . . .Aundrea Fudge
Casting Director. . . . . .Fran Cattaneo
Casting Assistant . . . . .Lydia Doyle
Stage Manager . . . . Shereen Hamilton
Production Manager . . . . .Adam Jefferys
Producer . . . . Ceri Lothian
Executive Producer . . . . Zena Tuitt-Collins
Associate Producer . . . . Clarisse Makundul Productions
Interim Producer . . . . .Humnah Abdullah
Costume Supervisor. . . . . .Bolu Dairo
PR. . . . . Nancy Poole PR
PR. . . . . .TGRG (The Girl in the Red Glasses)

CAST

SYDNEY SAINTÉ | MOTHER/MOTHER (MODERN DAY)

Sydney Sainté is a New York-born, London-based actor. After receiving her BFA in Drama from NYU's Tisch School of the Arts in 2014, she made her Off-Broadway debut in the world premiere of Roy Williams' play *Loneliness of the Long Distance Runner* at Atlantic Theater Company.

Credits include: *Black Cake* (Hulu) and *The Mallorca Files: Series 3* (Amazon). She is thrilled to be making her London stage debut in Nia Akilah Robinson's *The Great Privation*.

CHRISTIE FEWRY | CHARITY/CHARITY (MODERN DAY)

Christie Fewry is graduating from Rose Bruford College (South West) with an award-winning short film, and is now making her stage debut in *The Great Privation*.

ROMEO MIKA | CUFFEE/CUFFEE (MODERN DAY)

Romeo is a Bafta scholarship recipient and Open Door alumni. Since graduating, Romeo recently made his professional theatre debut with Mischief Theatre Company, in their National Tour of *Peter Pan Goes Wrong*.

Credits whilst training include: *The Leftovers, We Anchor in Hope, New Labour* and *The Children* (Short Film).

JACK GOULDBOURNE | JOHN/JOHN (MODERN DAY)

Jack has been acting since he was eleven. His professional debut was onstage as Iz in *Cargo* (Metal Rabbit Prod, Arcola Theatre) back in 2016. Since then, Jack has primarily worked on screen, with credits including Calum in *Fighting with my Family* (Seven Bucks, Channel 4 Films) and Norman Whaley in *Sister Boniface Mysteries* (BBC), so he now eagerly returns to the stage.

Jack's portrayal of characters like Nuro in *Secret Invasion* (Marvel Studios), Jimo Power in *Casualty* (BBC), Kris in *Holby City* (BBC), and Craig Megson in *As I Am* (Zebrafish Media) show his passion and ability to portray a diverse range of characters.

CREATIVE TEAM

WRITER | NIA AKILAH ROBINSON

Nia Akilah Robinson (She/her) is a playwright and actor who reps Harlem with all her might. She will have a London premiere of her play *The Great Privation*, at Theatre503. The Hearth is producing Nia's play *Push Party* at TheatreLab in New York City. In the fall, she will be a playwriting MFA candidate at David Geffen School of Drama at Yale. She is a graduating second-year playwright in the Juilliard School's Lila Acheson Wallace American Playwrights Program. Her work has been seen and developed with Steppenwolf Theatre, The Hearth, The New Group, Theatre503 (UK), The Ground Floor: Berkeley Repertory Theatre, Great Plains Theatre Conference, SPACE on Ryder Farm, Ensemble Studio Theatre, Waterwell, Classical Theatre of Harlem, Urbanite, and New Georges. She has been a MacDowell Fellow, Travis Bogard Eugene O'Neill Foundation Fellow, and a writer for PEN America and EST/Alfred P. Sloan Foundation (short play). Nia has had residencies at NYSAF and The Pocantico Center through YoungArts. Nia's work will be featured in the 2024 46th Bay Area Playwrights Festival, 2024 The Fire This Time Festival, was featured in the 2023 SPACE JAM @ Roundabout Theatre, and the 48th Samuel French Off-Off-Broadway Short Play Festival. She participated in the National Black Theatre Soul Series and received the 2023 Film & TV Mentorship by Mitzi Miller. She has been awarded 1st Place for the 2023 A is For Playwriting Contest, the Next Wave Initiative Lorraine Hansberry Writing Scholarship, a Miranda Family Fund Commission, and the NYSCA Grant (CCCADI). She is shortlisted for the 2023 Theatre503's International Playwriting Award. She was a finalist for the Audible Commission, the O'Neill National Playwrights Conference, and the Blue Ink Playwriting Award. She is a member or alumna of Ensemble Studio Theatre's Youngblood, I-73 at Page 73, The Orchard Project NYCGreenhouse, The Wish Collective, and TheBlackHERthePen. She is proudly represented by Alex Gold at Creative Artists Agency.

DIRECTOR | KALUNGI SSEBANDEKE

Kalungi Ssebandeke trained as an Actor at Guildhall School of Music and Drama where he was made BAFTA Scholar 2017-2019 plus a Josephine Hart Scholar. After working as a Writer/Director and lead facilitator at White City Youth Theatre, working as a director-in-residence and drama teacher at a leading independent school and directing Martin Crimp's *Attempts on Her Life* at Bristol School of Acting, Kalungi made his professional directorial debut with *Meetings* by Mustapha Matura, 2023's winner of the JMK Directing Award. He is currently the Carne Associate Director at Theatre503.

Acting credits include: *We Need New Names* (New Perspectives and Fifth Word); The titular role in *Othello* (The Watermill); *Duchess of Malfi* (Almeida); *Blood Knot* (Orange Tree); *The 14th Tale* by Inua Ellams (Fuel Theatre); *Image of an Unknown Young Woman* (The Gate Theatre); *We are Proud to Present...*(The Bush Theatre); *One Monkey Don't Stop No Show* (Kiln/Sheffield Theatres plus national Tour); *There's Only One Wayne Matthews* (Sheffield Theatres); *Skins* (Channel 4 in an episode written by Daniel Kaluuya); *Columbite Tantalite* (Young Vic/ Guardian and directed by Chiwetel Ejiofor).

Writing credits include: *Prodigal* (Orange Tree); *Assata Taught Me* (The Gate Theatre, directed by Lynette Linton); *Marriage Plan* (Euras Films).

Kalungi is also a musician and his debut album Katugende is available on all streaming sites under the name Kalungi Fresh.

SET AND COSTUME DESIGNER | RUTH BADILA

Ruth trained at the University of the Arts, Wimbledon, graduating in 2020. She has since landed the role of Associate Assistant Designer at the Kiln Theatre. Working and learning from a range of amazing creatives, mentored by Tom Piper. She hopes to contribute and respond innovatively to the rapid change of the industry. Whilst also thinking of ways theatre can become much more accessible and representative. She has recently finished her year-long role at the National Theatre as an Assistant Designer.

LIGHTING DESIGNER | CHUMA EMEMBOLU

Lighting Designer Chuma Emembolu trained with the Royal Shakespeare Company, under the Lighting Designer. He has worked on numerous Offie commended productions including *Great Expectations* (The Playground Theatre); *Macbeth the Musical* (The White Bear Theatre); *For Black Boys Who Considered Suicide When The Hue Got To Heavy* (New Diorama Theatre) and an Offie nominated production *The Good Dad* (The Old Red Lion Theatre).

Other Lighting credits include: *Sir John in Love* (Opera Holland Park); *Semele* (Blackheath Halls); *Around the world in 80 days* (Theatre by the lake); *Comedy of Errors* (Shakespeare North Playhouse); *The ShoeMaker* (Wales Millennium Centre); *Six of Calais* (Royal Academy of Music); *The Throne* (Charing Cross Theatre); *Aspern Papers, L'enfant, Poison Passion* and *Purification* (Royal Academy of Music); *The Night Woman* (The Other Palace); *Maggie and Ted* (Garrick Theatre); *Don Juan* (Hoxton Hall Theatre); *The Exceptional Case of Whizz and Drex* (The Old Red Lion Theatre).

SOUND DESIGNER & COMPOSER | JOSÉ GUILLERMO PUELLO

José Guillermo Puello is a Composer and Sound Designer based in Manchester, originally from the Dominican Republic. Since graduating from the University of Manchester with a PhD in Composition in 2015, he has worked in theatre, dance and concert hall. As a Sound Designer: *Meetings* (Orange Tree Theatre); *Dream School* (The Space); *Stray Dogs* (Theatre503); *There's no Planet B* (Theatre Deli); *Legacy* (Royal Exchange Theatre). As an Assistant Sound Designer: *The Human Body* (Donmar Warehouse); *Rock, Paper, Scissor* (Sheffield Theatres).

Concert hall commissions include: Northern Opera Group; OperaNorth, Manchester Chamber Choir, MusicAbierta, soundSCAPE Exchange, Dominican Republic National Youth Orchestra, Fourth Wall Ensemble, Manchester Camerata.

Dance Credits include: *Lonely Cities* (Rambert Studio); *Hiatus* (Contact Theatre).

MOVEMENT DIRECTOR | YEMURAI ZVARAYA

Yemurai; a versatile, multidisciplinary artist from Zimbabwe, trained at a Theatre company, specialises in Movement Direction, infused with influences from hip hop and commercial dance. Her innovative approach earned her an Offie nomination for *I Love Acting but F*ck This Industry* at Theatre Peckham, showcasing her unique perspective.

Assistant Choreographer for *Stranger Things* in the West End, Yemurai's impact transcends her solo work, contributing to the commercial dance and hip hop scenes. She balances her career as a dancer and performer while passionately carving out her creative space, driven by dedication to individual projects and collaborative endeavours on stage.

CASTING DIRECTOR | FRAN CATTANEO

Fran is a freelance Senior Casting Assistant and Casting Director, working across stage and screen, having worked in the offices of Dan Hubbard, James and Rosie Pearson, Stuart Burt and Heather Basten.

As a Casting Assistant for Theatre, her credits include; *Red Pitch*, *Fair Play* and *House of Ife* (Bush Theatre); Kwame Kwei-Armah's *Beneatha's Place* (Young Vic) and Jamie Lloyd's *Sunset Boulevard* (Savoy Theatre).

As a Casting Director for theatre, her credits include; Selina Thompson's *Twine* (Yard Theatre); *This Might Not Be It* (Bush Theatre); *Dorothy A Play* (ICA) and the upcoming UK Premiere of *The Bleeding Tree* (Southwark Playhouse).

CASTING ASSISTANT | LYDIA DOYLE

Lydia is a freelance Casting Assistant and Writer. She is currently assisting Fran Cattaneo across various theatre and screen projects.

VOICE AND DIALECT COACH | AUNDREA FUDGE

Aundrea Fudge is an Accent/Dialect and Speech Coach from New York. She completed her MFA in Voice Studies from the Royal Central School of Speech and Drama in 2018 and is currently based in London where she currently teaches and runs accent workshops for The Royal Central School of Speech and Drama, The Royal Academy of Dramatic Arts, Bristol Old Vic Theatre School, and Guildhall School of Music and Drama.

Theatre includes: *Clyde's* (Donmar Warehouse); *Choir Boy* (Bristol Old Vic); *A View From The Bridge* (UK Tour/ Headlong); *Meetings, Yelloman* (Orange Tree); *Start Swimming!* (Young Vic); *Once on this Island* (Regents Park Open Air); *Blackout Songs* (Hampstead); *Bootycandy* (Gate Theatre); *Refilwe* (Bernie Grant Arts Centre); *Cinderella* (Brixton House); *Driving Miss Daisy* (Barn Theatre) and *Bring it on! The Musical* (Southbank).

Film includes: *Bernard & The Genie; Locked In-Film* and *Wheel of Time*. TV includes: *Andor* (Season 2)

PRODUCTION MANAGER | ADAM JEFFERYS

Adam is a Lighting Designer and Production Manager from Essex. Previously, he was the Technical Manager of the New Diorama Theatre. Recent work includes: *My Father's Fable* (Bush Theatre); *The Bleeding Tree* (Southwark Playhouse); *Murder In The Dark* (UK Tour); *Elephant* (Bush Theatre); *It Is I, Seagull* (UK Tour); *Soon* (Summerhall Festival); *Pilot* (Summerhall Festival); *Philosophy of The World* (Cambridge Junction); *After The Act* (New Diorama); *War & Culture* (New Diorama); *Under The Kundè Tree* (Southwark Playhouse); *Jekyll and Hyde* (Derby Theatre); *Project Dictator* (New Diorama & Edinburgh); *Everything Has Changed* (Tour & Edinburgh) and *Dorian* (Reading Rep). For more of Adam's work please visit his website: www.adamjefferys.com.

STAGE MANAGER | SHEREEN HAMILTON

Shereen is a dedicated and versatile Creative Practitioner. Alongside her BA and MA in Theatre and Performance, specialising in the intersectionality of race and gender in theatrical representations, Shereen has trained and worked as a Producer, Director, Actor, Stage Manager and Facilitator. Her area of work centres around intersectional identities on stage and using theatre as a vehicle of education. Shereen has worked with many award winning venues: Assistant Director on *Seven Methods of Killing Kylie Jenner* (The Royal Court Theatre); Director on Jamie Hale's *CRIPtic Pit Party* (The Barbican); Producer on *#BlackIs...* (Company Three / New Diorama); Creative Producer on *SAMSKARA* (The Yard Theatre); Stage Manager on Directors development R&D at Headlong Theatre, Community Connector on Artist Development Programme at Southbank Centre and Production Trainee on *Taskmaster* at Avalon Productions/Channel 4.

PRODUCER | CERI LOTHIAN

Ceri started her career as Resident Assistant Producer at Theatre503, working on new writing productions that included the World Premieres of *And Then Come The Nightjars* by Bea Roberts (2016 National Tour), and *Rotterdam* by Jon Brittain (Olivier Award Winner, 2017). She was Associate Producer and General Manager at Deus Ex Machina Productions from 2016-2021, where credits include *RIDE* (Garrick Theatre, 2021); *The Secret Diary of Adrian Mole Age 13 3/4: The Musical* (Ambassadors Theatre, 2019); *DUST* by Milly Thomas (Trafalgar Studio 2 2018, New York Theatre Workshop, 2019); *Spring Awakening* (Hope Mill Theatre, 2018); Stephen Schwartz' *Working* (Southwark Playhouse, 2017). She is currently the Producer at Theatre503, where credits include *Milk & Gall, Moreno, The Boys Are Kissing* and *A Woman Walks Into a Bank*. Ceri has taken part in Stage One workshops, and is an Ambassador for Inspiring The Future of Theatre with SOLT and UK Theatre.

ASSOCIATE PRODUCER | CLARISSE MAKUNDUL PRODUCTIONS

Clarisse Makundul Productions is a new theatre production company dedicated to presenting diverse voices.

Clarisse Makundul is a performer, playwright, and producer. She is also a member of the Orange Tree Writers Collective 2023/24.

Producing credits include: the world premiere of *Under the Kundè Tree* (***** "A tremendous piece of theatre" The Reviews Hub, Offie nominated for Lead Performance, The BBTAS nominated for Supporting Actor), directed by Ebenezer Bamgboye at Southwark Playhouse; the UK premiere of *One Who Wants To Cross* (**** The Stage, **** The Guardian, **** Reviews Hub, **** ReviewsGate, in the Guardian's ten best theatre shows of 2023), directed by Alice Hamilton at the Finborough Theatre; the staged reading of *Facing Mother* by award-winning playwright, actor and director Jean-René Lemoine at the Park Theatre.

INTERIM PRODUCER | HUMNAH ABDULLAH

Humnah is the Interim Producer at Theatre503, with *The Great Privation* as her first credit in the role. Previously she was Assistant Producer of Theatre503, where her credits included *A Woman Walks Into a Bank*, and was Lead Producer on their Spring Short Season 2024. Humnah is also Lead Producer for Pink Milk Theatre, where her credits include Lead Producer of *Naughty: 2022 UK Tour* (Hen and Chickens Theatre, The Kings Arms, Wrecking Ball Arts Centre, The Other Room 2022) by Andrew Houghton and across all iterations for *A Splash of Milk* (Hen and Chickens Theatre 2022, The Hope Theatre 2022 and Omnibus Theatre 2023) by Sami Sumaria. She is also Founder of

Humnah Abdullah Productions, a company setup to champion joyful intersectionality in new writing. Humnah is thrilled to be supported by the Stage One Bursary Scheme for New Producers, and is on their Bridge The Gap programme

EXECUTIVE PRODUCER | ZENA TUITT-COLLINS
Zena Tuitt-Collins is a trustee at Theatre503 and executive produced *J'Ouvert* by Yasmin Joseph at Theatre503 in 2019.

COSTUME SUPERVISOR | BOLU DAIRO
Bolu is a London-based set and costume designer who trained at The Royal Central School of Speech and Drama.

She is driven by the collaborative process and seeing creative visions come to life.

Theatre503 is at the forefront of identifying and nurturing new voices at the very start of their careers and launching them into the industry. They stage more early career playwrights than any other theatre in the world – with over 120 writers premiered each year from festivals of short pieces to full length productions, resulting in employment for over 1,000 freelance artists through their year-round programme.

Theatre503 provides a diverse pipeline of talent resulting in modern classics like **The Mountaintop** by Katori Hall and **Rotterdam** by Jon Brittain – both Olivier Award winners – to future classics like Yasmin Joseph's **J'Ouvert**, winner of the 2020 James Tait Black Prize and transferred to the West End/BBC Arts and **Wolfie** by Ross Willis, winner of the 2020 Writers Guild Award for Best New Play. Writers who began their creative life at Theatre503 are now writing for the likes of *One Day*, *The Crown*, *Succession*, *Doctor Who*, *Killing Eve* and *Normal People* and every single major subsidised theatre in the country now boasts a new play by a writer who started at Theatre503.

Theatre503 TEAM

Artistic Director . . . . Lisa Spirling
Executive Director . . . . Emily Carewe
Literary Manager . . . . .Steve Harper
Producer . . . . Ceri Lothian
General Manager . . . . Emily Dickson
Carne Associate Director . . . . Kalungi Ssebandeke
Literary Associate . . . . .Lauretta Barrow
Technical Coordinator . . . . .Paul Kaiba
Box Office Manager . . . . .Blair McAlpine
Marketing Officer . . . . .Millie Whittam
Interim Producer . . . . .Humnah Abdullah

Theatre503 BOARD

Erica Whyman OBE (Chair)
Royce Bell (Co-Vice Chair)
Emma Rees (Co-Vice Chair)
Eleanor Lloyd
Jack Tilbury
Ollie Raggett
Roy Williams OBE

Zena Tuitt-Collins
Joshua Chua
Naomi Kerbel
Cerian Walsh
Kandy Rohmann
Pippa Hill
Tian Brown-Sampson
(Associate Trustee)

Theatre503's work would not be possible without the support of the following individuals, trusts and organisations.

We are particularly grateful to Philip and Christine Carne for their long-term support of our International Playwriting Award, the 503 Five and Carne Associate.

Theatre503 would like to thank Philip and Christine Carne, sponsors of the Carne Prize, and Concord Theatricals for their generous support of the Theatre503 International Playwriting Award. Thanks to all the 2023 Theatre503 International Playwriting Award Readers: Almiro Andrade, Tian Brown-Sampson, Lisa Cagnacci, Lou Corben, Sujana Crawford, Amy Bethan Evans, Adam Goodall, William Gregory, Neil Grutchfield, Isabelle Kassam, Erick Kwashie, Tom Latter, Kyle Marsh, Robbie Nestor, Nika Obydzinski, Gugulethu Oka Mseleku, Shefali Parmar, Fatima Serghini, Andrew Skipper, Audrey Thayer, Pravin Wilkins, Beth Wilson.

Additional thanks to Adïam Yemane, the counselors Natasha Preville (The Ascension Agency) and Aisha Gordon-Hiles BSc, MSc, PGDIP, MBACP ACCRED.

503Patrons: Ayla & Jon Hill, Carol Rahn & David Baxter, Catharine Roos, Eilene Davidson, Eric Bensaude, Freddie Hutchins & Oliver Rawlins, Gaskell & Jennifer Jacobs, Geraldine Sharpe-Newton, Jack Tilbury/Plann, Jules Oakshett, Laura Riddeck, Lisa Swinney, Lou Wilks & Tom Gowans, Louise Rawlins, Marcus Markou, Marianne Badrichani, Matthew Marren, Nick Hern Books, Pam Alexander & Roger Booker, Pippa Hill, Reed Smith LLP, Robert O'Dowd, Sally O'Neill, Sean Winnett, Simon Godwin, The Bell Family, The Bloor Family, United Agents and all our 503Friends and Share the Drama supporters.

503 Slate Philanthropic Co-Producers: Cas & Philip Donald, Concord Music Group, Inc, Eilene Davidson, Gordon Bloor, Hania Farrell, Jean Doumanian/Peony NY LLC, Kater Gordon Productions Ltd, Kofi Owusu Bempah, Lucas Achkar, Marcus Markou, Ocourant Ltd, Royce Bell, Trish Wadley Productions, Peter Wilson Productions.

Arts Council England Grants for the Arts, Backstage Trust, Cockayne Grants for the Arts, Concord Theatricals (503 Playwriting Award), Garrick Charitable Trust, Gregory Annenberg Weingarten, GRoW @ Annenberg, Theatres Trust, The de Laszlo Foundation, Old Possum's Practical Trust, The Foyle Foundation, The Orseis Trust (503Five), Wandsworth Borough Council.

Our ongoing thanks and gratitude to Three Cheers Pub Co. for our home above The Latchmere Pub.

CHARACTERS

CHARITY & CHARITY (MODERN DAY) – She/Her. *Black. 16. Of Darker skin tone*. 1832, funny, busy, intense. Modern day, very hyperactive and bubbly. Slightly hood-whimsical. A very physically comedic actor.

MOTHER & MOTHER (MODERN DAY) (MISSY FREEMAN) – She/Her. *Black. 34*. Six feet tall. 1832, Private. In Control. Funny.

Modern day, seemingly open and older. Suspicious of others. Loud.

JOHN & JOHN (MODERN DAY) – He/Him/They/Them. *White. 25. Redhead. Blonde is fine too*. 1832, Outgoing. Lacks empathy. avoidant. modern day, gives musical theater energy.

JANITOR & CUFFEE (MODERN DAY) – He/Him. *Black. 32. Tall in stature and presence*. 1832, Loud. Unapologetic. Bold. Modern day, huggable. Lovable. Shy. Silly. Just wants everyone to have STRUCTURED FUN.

SETTING

African Baptist Church's Graveyard and a cabin behind the Graveyard in Philadelphia (built in 1931).

TIME

Time interchanges between...
October 21st–October 23rd of **1832** &
July 2nd–July 4th of **"The Year You Are Currently In"**

NOTES ON SCRIPT

Full stops indicate a small breath

Text in bold should be stressed

AUTHOR'S NOTES

– **The dialogue should run at the speed of lighting. The more air the more we lose the play. Mother, Charity, John, Cuffee are fighters.**

– There may be confusion that arises between when you are "modern" & and when you "aren't". That is the point.

– A countdown clock is needed for the play.

– Do I think we are our ancestors? No.

– *Moses* is Charity's father & Mother's husband.

– **The graves do not have "gravestones".**

– **Include a box outside of the theater space, labeled, "If you are Black, take this". Please include a sheet of paper rolled up and tied with a ribbon. It is a gift. Its contents are on the last page of the play.**

What is our responsibility to time?
What stories bloom in the gaps of the unknown?
How do fragments turn into nightmares?

The play is inspired by Harriet A. Washington, Gary B. Nash,
and Schomburg Library research.

I also, want to thank Matthew, Zena, Kalungi, Evern, Arminda,
Heather, Dr. Deborah, Renee, Tommi, Vivienne, Adesuwa,
The Bay Area Playwrights Conference, Alex Gold,
and of course all of Theatre503 (I am forever grateful for you & to you).

And most importantly, Mom and Dad, you both are my heart.

Scene One

(There is a digital clock above stage left, which bleeps 72:00:00 over and over at the top of the play. October 21st, 1832. African Baptist Church's Graveyard in Philadelphia. It is one in the morning. **CHARITY** *and* **MOTHER** *sit at opposite ends of Moses' grave. Visually, the audience should not understand that we are at a gravesite.)*

CHARITY. Mommie.

MOTHER. Yes?

CHARITY. I miss food.

MOTHER. Yes. I do, as well.

CHARITY. Are you well?

MOTHER. New.

.

Empty.

CHARITY. Cold?

MOTHER. Are you these things?

CHARITY. Hungry?

Sad?

Cold?

I'm also angry.

MOTHER. I gather that. Talk about something else Charity.

CHARITY. Do you think I could be an apprentice?

MOTHER. Where?

CHARITY. I thought you could help me figure that out.

MOTHER. You don't want to take over my business?

CHARITY. If you really want me to, I will.

MOTHER. You hate preparing the candy pulls.

Even though mine are the best in town.

CHARITY. WILL WE EVER BE ABLE TO EAT AGAIN?

MOTHER. Charity, sh!

CHARITY. *(Like her perception of a dictator.)* A BAN OF ALL DAIRY, FRUITS, AND VEGETABLES IN THE CITY OF PHILADELPHIA.

NO DRINKING COLD WATER.

HEAT YOUR WATER

HEAT IT.

MOTHER. Let's play the quiet game.

CHARITY. No.

MOTHER. *(Closes eyes.)*

(Beat.)

CHARITY. Mom.

Mom.

Mommy.

Mom.

Mom.

Mommy.

Mom.

Do you know what day it is?

This October?

MOTHER. The 21st. October 21st, 1832.

CHARITY. *(Sings a song reminiscent of "Papa Was A Rollin' Stone" but innocently.*)*

And *this* was the day that my daddy died. You think any bodies are left in these graves besides/

MOTHER. /No, not many.

CHARITY. Daddy got to be next to the tree. He must be happy.

MOTHER. It cost extra.

Twenty for the preparation and the pine box.

Five to be next to the tree.

CHARITY. Are you resting your eyes?

MOTHER. Does it look like I am?

CHARITY. Yes.

MOTHER. You'll be the eyes.

I'll be the ears.

(Points to herself.) Bat. *(Points to **CHARITY**.)* Owl.

CHARITY. You can't hear that well.

MOTHER. I heard you sneak out last Friday past curfew.

CHARITY. What?

---

* A licence to produce *The Great Privation* does not include a performance licence for any third-party or copyrighted music. Licensees should create an original composition or use music in the public domain. For further information, please see the Music and Third-Party Materials Use Note on page iii.

MOTHER. What?

CHARITY. I did not.

MOTHER. Oh. My ears must be *off*.

CHARITY. Agreed.

MOTHER. I could get fined if they caught you.

CHARITY. *(Okay you caught me.)* Me, Noah and/

MOTHER. /Abel snuck into African Baptists' basement.

CHARITY. Did you follow me?!

MOTHER. I made sure to stick around just in case you got caught.

CHARITY. OK.

MOTHER. And I saw you and Noah, Abel, **and Faith** drinking whiskey.

I wondered where you got whiskey from Charity, your father's cabinet perhaps?

CHARITY. …

MOTHER. *(Opening her eyes.)* Oh, no more talking?

(Closing her eyes.) I was enjoying myself.

CHARITY. Why did you wait until now to say these words?

MOTHER. Your father falling ill, nothing more.

CHARITY. I kissed Noah.

MOTHER. And Faith.

CHARITY. MOM.

MOTHER. If word got out.

CHARITY. I know.

MOTHER. Okay.

CHARITY. I'm sorry.

MOTHER. For?

CHARITY. Being foolish.

MOTHER. There are eyes everywhere.

CHARITY. Even now?

MOTHER. Yes.

.

.

.

Though, the night guard is absent.

CHARITY. Strange.

> (**MOTHER** *opens her eyes.*)

MOTHER. Before your father died, he told me about these metal cages that people in Scotland put over the pine boxes to lock the bodies in.

CHARITY. That would be nice.

MOTHER. Right?!

CHARITY. You think white people have those?

MOTHER. No. Most of their locks are invisible.

CHARITY. How do we get those locks?

MOTHER. Turn white.

CHARITY. Pass.

MOTHER. Exactly that.

CHARITY. *(Random.)* I plan to marry a caterer, so I never have to touch the kitchen.

MOTHER. A cook, you mean?

CHARITY. What's on the menu tonight, I'd ask?

> (*Suffering because of the food ban.*)

Soup? Bread? Rice? Waaah Waaaah.

I know we'd be eating the same boring food night after night.

But it's okay, because my meals would be prepared by a COOK, you see MAMA?

(*New thought.*) You can't even make your candy pulls anymore since lemons are banned.

So even if I marry, what he goin' make us now?

A bowl of nothin'?

It's awful.

MOTHER. A cook ain't goin' to want to cook when he gets home from cookin'.

When the catering businesses open back up, you'll have to eat leftovers from the kitchens.

Why you talkin' about marrying when you want to apprentice anyway?

Focus on yourself.

Then worry about that other stuff.

CHARITY. (*WAAAT, DON'T GET MARRIED?!*) MOMMIE ARE YOU SICK?

MOTHER. (*We're in a graveyard.*) Don't joke here.

.

.

Live your life the way you choose.

I want that for you.

Daddy wanted that for you.

CHARITY. Guess what I brought with me to keep us occupied?

MOTHER. Moses' old newspaper from New York City.

> (**CHARITY** *digs through a bag.*)

Clouding your mind with the world's old news.

That your daddy didn't want you lookin' at.

You couldn't wait a DAY Charity

> **CHARITY**.
> *(Opens the newspaper.)*
> *(Upon discovery.)* MOM.
> STOP. MOM.

MOTHER. What?!

CHARITY. THERE'S A WIDOWER

WHO HAD AN AD OUT ABOUT

FINDING A WIFE.

He was looking for someone

Sweet

Quiet

MOTHER. I'm out of the running.

CHARITY. You can't marry again.

It wouldn't be right.

MOTHER. I'm not being serious.

I'm thirty-four anyway.

Should've died already.

CHARITY. You're a wapper.

MOTHER. Do you know what a wapper means?

CHARITY. *(Lying.)* Yes.

MOTHER. Look it up when you get home silly.

CHARITY. *(Reading from the newspaper.)* Knows French.

MOTHER. He's asking for a lot.

CHARITY. There's fifteen more requirements.

MOTHER. Bleh.

CHARITY. Apparently, a group of local women came to see him.

And laughed in his face.

This is all in Connecticut by the way.

MOTHER. Oh. That's awful.

CHARITY. I was hoping Daddy would have another newspaper from the Freedom News.

MOTHER. You need a subscription to receive the paper.

CHARITY. Can we get one?

MOTHER. Do you have "get one" money?

CHARITY. I have a dollar saved.

MOTHER. I think they went out of business, Charity.

And you'd need two more dollars.

CHARITY. There are newspaper companies here too.

MOTHER. *(Referring to her and Moses.)* We don't like the way they run their business.

CHARITY. NO. You and Daddy don't like them because the editors attend white churches.

MOTHER. Maybe. Maybe not.

CHARITY. *(Making fun.)* Maybe. Maybe not.

MOTHER. There are African churches.

Yet they attend the white churches?

The white churches that they aren't allowed to sit within.

What does that say about their writing?

Who is their newspaper really for?

(A loud sound of gushing water.)

CHARITY. What's that?!

MOTHER. They're cleaning.

Washing the streets.

CHARITY. Cleaning it of the Cholera?

MOTHER. Yes. Exactly.

CHARITY. The mortality list is getting longer and longer.

MOTHER. Less cases here now, than in New York City. *(Looking off.)* You see him approaching?

CHARITY. Yes.

Do we have a plan?

MOTHER. We just know what we are not going to allow to happen.

CHARITY. Right.

*(We hear **JOHN** entering.)*

(He stops far off, carrying an empty burlap sack, long enough for a human body, and a shovel.)

JOHN. Mrs. Freeman?

MOTHER. I am she.

Mrs. Freeman.

JOHN. And your name, little one?

CHARITY. I'm sixteen.

JOHN. Sixteen is a great age to be.

  My name is John.

MOTHER. You're at a grave for **Afric peoples**, you do realize?

JOHN. Yes.

MOTHER. Do you come here often?

JOHN. My colleagues do.

  It would be my first time at this location.

MOTHER. Oh.

  Well.

  My husband was buried here this afternoon.

  Our reasoning for being here.

JOHN. I see.

> (**JOHN** *steps forward slightly.*)

MOTHER. *(Hands raising.)* Oh.

  Sir.

  I'm praying.

  For my husband's safe journey back to Sierra Leone.

  To be with his distant family.

JOHN. Of course.

  How long do you plan to pray?

MOTHER. The journey to Sierra Leone is a long one.

  Have you ever been?

JOHN. You understand why I'm here, correct?

MOTHER. I know why you're here.

  Correct.

You know why I'm here. Correct?

JOHN. To pray.

If that is the truth.

I can respect that, as I am a Christian myself.

MOTHER. Have you ever lost anyone close to you?

JOHN. My father. I was your daughter's age when I lost him.

MOTHER. So, you understand?

JOHN. There's a difference

I don't pray at night over his grave.

I pray at home.

MOTHER. It was my husband's last request of us.

To see him off.

JOHN. Oh.

I can understand.

Somewhat.

MOTHER. Thank you.

JOHN. My father had us make a death mask for him.

It's a tradition in my family.

MOTHER. A death mask?

I'm not sure I follow.

JOHN. When the men in the family die the women make clay masks of their faces.

MOTHER. Oh.

JOHN. *(Focused.)* Well.

Is there a time?

A time which I may return?

MOTHER. *(Masking offense.)* Return?

Oh.

I do not have an answer to your question.

JOHN. Do you plan to pray at night?

Again?

MOTHER. I plan to be a dutiful wife to my late husband.

JOHN. That's all you can be.

.

.

Make sure to not get caught by the police.

Ladies shouldn't be out so late.

MOTHER. *(Referring to offstage.)* You should take your tools back to wherever they came from alright?

JOHN. *(Warning.)* **For tonight.**

I will do as you wish.

MOTHER.

.

.

.

(This is code.) The journey to Africa takes a long while.

JOHN.

.

.

.

(Hears the code.) Shorten it.

　　　*(**JOHN** exits.)*

CHARITY. Colleagues.

What does he mean colleagues?

What does that mean?

What does colleagues mean?

MOTHER. He's a student at college.

CHARITY. I thought White people take bodies to torture us further.

Like what they did to Nat Turner last year.

(Clarifying.) But students are the ones who take our bodies?

MOTHER. Yes.

CHARITY. Students studying what?

MOTHER. Charity.

CHARITY. Students studying what?

How do you know he's really a/

MOTHER. /Breathe.

CHARITY. Why?

You want me to ask my friends?

They'll tell me.

MOTHER. Your friends don't know a thing.

CHARITY. *(Standing.)* I can ask him myself. I'll do it.

MOTHER. Sure, you can.

CHARITY. (**CHARITY** *stays in place.)* Why didn't you tell me this before?!

MOTHER. I didn't want it to be true.

Not for US.

It couldn't be.

CHARITY. *(Revelation.)* They do to us, what I've done to a
    frog in science class.

> *(**MOTHER** lays over the grave. Puts her arm
> around it, and sobs.)*

> *(**CHARITY** grabs the newspaper and reads. A
> slow dim. **CHARITY** and **MOTHER** exit. The
> tree glows. The soil glows. A timer appears.
> A countdown clock appears. We see 47:00:00
> countdown to 46:59:45.)*

Scene Two

(July 2nd of "whatever year we are currently in". It is mid-afternoon. Upstage of the graveyard we imagine a small camp counselors lunch cabin. A production assistant wheels in a cart with a coffee maker on the top deck, and a refrigerator on the bottom. **JOHN** *enters followed by* **CHARITY** *and* **MOTHER**, *carrying lunch trays and folded chairs.)*

JOHN. F these kids.

CHARITY. F 'em.

JOHN. How am I reported? At a sleepaway camp?!

MOTHER. It's happened to me.

One more strike and I'm fired.

My reports from the Harlem location carried over here.

JOHN. And now I have to tip toe around Timmy like he isn't a **crim-i-nal.**

CHARITY. I know.

JOHN. **CUFFEE**, **calls me in.**

Actin' like my superior.

(By the way.) Cuffee was a camp counselor

Just a year ago.

What did *he* have to do to get promoted?

MOTHER. *Um.*

JOHN. I tell Timmy to "shut up".

I didn't say "f off TIMMY", which I wanted to do, I really did.

Timmy pulled Imani's braids.

Imani stuck her finger up Timmy's nose.

RIGHTFULLY SO.

I saw it all.

I mean, I wasn't expecting her to make that move.

She seems **timider** than the others.

But GO IMANI.

They run to me.

YOU SAW Charity.

Imani tries to speak.

TIMMY speaks OVER IMANI

Which is to be expected.

WHITE BOYS TRYING TO TALK OVER BLACK GIRLS AM I RIGHT?

CHARITY.   **MOTHER.**
Oh/   I/

JOHN. /AND IM LIKE SHUT UP TIMMY

You know his mom has frozen breast milk for him in the kitchen's fridge?

He's nine.

You know that right?

CHARITY. Yes.

JOHN. I mean.

> *(Takes a bite of sandwich.)*

Wait, I have a question.

CHARITY. Yeah?

JOHN. Has anyone been farting more than usual?

I feel like the kitchen staff puts laxatives in the...

>   (**MOTHER** *slowly spits out her food.*)

Wait.

I'm so sorry.

Oh my god.

This isn't a good day for me.

I do have to tell you both something.

Don't hate me.

CHARITY. What?

JOHN. Cuffee asked me

What were we doing in the room

With the kids

For that to happen.

Between Imani and Timmy.

Because he said incidents typically happen during unstructured activities.

And I said we let them have **free time** in the room.

And/

CHARITY. /Oh no.

JOHN. He looked at our Group 2 schedule and asked why we weren't giving the STEM lesson like we were supposed to during that time block. He said it could've all been avoided, if we were, you know, doing what we were supposed to be doing.

MOTHER. So.

You're saying we might get reported?

All of us?

JOHN. …

CHARITY. We're not teachers I don't understand.

    This is sleepaway camp.

    It's supposed to be fun.

    It's their second day here.

    We'll do the lesson.

    John…

        (Looks up and rolls her eyes.)

    I need a good recommendation from this job.

    It's my first job ever.

JOHN. I'm sorry.

CHARITY. *(Looking at* **MOTHER**.*)* You won't get fired, mom.

JOHN. MOM?

CHARITY. That's my mom.

    Couldn't you tell?

JOHN. Oh my god.

    I didn't want to be the racist asshole who thought you just looked alike.

MOTHER. That's my daughter, yeah.

    I said that in training.

JOHN. Oh.

    You **did.**

    I feel like I can go clean this up with him.

    I'll figure it out.

    (Looks at watch and gathers things.) I'll meet you in the cafeteria to pick up the kids in ten.

(**JOHN** *exits.*)

CHARITY. Can I have my phone back? We're on break.

MOTHER. You know you can't have it back.

CHARITY. It's already viral. We can't do anything about it.

MOTHER. Can you take it off your page?

CHARITY. I did. People are still sharing it.

MOTHER. I report each video. But, they keep multiplying. TikTok is the bane of my existence. I had your grandma report it too.

CHARITY. Grandma doesn't know how to work an app like that.

MOTHER. Charity.

CHARITY. Mom, you made another account under grandma's name. Just admit it.

MOTHER. You vandalized school property ON CAMERA.

CHARITY. You're taking the systems side.

MOTHER. No.

CHARITY. You're not taking the people's side.

MOTHER. No PEOPLES. Just YOU.

(**CHARITY** *holds up the Black power fist.*)

CHARITY. POWER TO THE PEOPLE.

MOTHER. Who you doing it to? It's only us up in here!

(**CHARITY** *puts down the fist.*)

Charity, I've been PRAYING they don't expel you. Your job is to do good work here this summer. Do the summer project they assigned as punishment for your actions. Don't LIKE, SHARE, COMMENT UNDER, or re-TikTok any other re-shares! Stay out of the limelight.

And write the apology letter to the janitor who had to paint over your mess. Did you do that? The meeting's before you know it!

CHARITY.   **Yes ma. And see, it** was too late to "expel me" because I did it on the last day of school. I have a business mindset. I'm smart. *(Does a funny TikTok dance move.)* Look at my brain.

MOTHER. Don't do nothing like you did at school **here.** Just don't.

CHARITY. I get it. We're here for grandma anyway.

MOTHER. To help her have an easy transition. I'm already sad about it. Please don't make me sadder.

CHARITY. *(Inhales twice and then speaks.)* The air is cleaner up here, but I find it harder to breathe. What a strange sensation.

> *(The leaves on the weeping tree turn red gradually and fall off looking like dripping blood.* **CHARITY** *and* **MOTHER** *see it (as if through a window), and walk to the graveyard, upon both of them touching the leaves on the floor, it becomes night two, a dreadful night in 1832.)*

Scene Three

(October 22nd, 1832. It is three in the morning. The clock glows at 20:00:00.)

CHARITY. JOHN GON' COME HERE

AND IMMA TAKE HIS LITTLE SHOVEL

AND I'M GON' KNOCK HIM OVER THE HEAD WITH IT.

MOTHER. *(With hyper speed and focus.)* If it comes to it

You won't do anything

I will do it

I was talking to Ms. Bea in the alleyway

While you was in school

She said

Half the people here don't want to believe that

It's real

The grave robbing

And the other half clearly know it's real

But, they don't have enough people

Who want to

You know

Fight back.

It's the church people

Our church people

Who would never believe our own

Church guard would

Take money from these resurrectionists.

(New note.) The ones who believe in what's going on
are –

The ones burying their loved ones

At the public grave

They know for sure it's real

In some ways it's the more wealthy

Black folks

Against

The poor Black folks

I don't know.

I feel like it's always been that way.

> (**CHARITY** *takes out a cloth with some bread.*)

MOTHER. Charity

We ate dinner three hours ago.

And you're still hungry?

> (**CHARITY** *nods.*)

Don't eat here.

Go eat on the other side of the tree.

We can't have crumbs on your father's grave.

(About the bread.) Save some, Charity there's a shortage.

> (**CHARITY** *sits at the other side of the tree.*)

CHARITY. Why don't we visit grandma's grave?

It would be nice.

I think

Right?

To visit.

MOTHER. Your grandmother and I were not close.

Like us.

CHARITY. She met me when I was a baby, you said.

MOTHER. Out of respect.

Yes.

CHARITY. Say more.

MOTHER. Your grandmother raised me for nine years before

I was sold to serve in the house on Franklin Street

The side of the street we never walk on

Because she had three other children she couldn't afford to take care of

Her and father were paid off for my labor.

Apparently, the Quakers helped make that happen.

One of those societies, you know 'em.

Which is why I don't like them very much either.

I worked until I was eighteen.

And that's why I swore I'd never do it again.

Work for whites.

And I'd make my own way

With my own business

That's also when I got serious with your father and pregnant with you.

CHARITY. Why do you wait to tell me the truth about your life?

I get little bits of truth each year I get older.

MOTHER. Apparently, it's a "mom" thing.

CHARITY. We must make it to three days with Daddy untouched.

MOTHER. And we will.

CHARITY. For the spiritual trip to Africa?

MOTHER. Yes, Stinky.

Bring out the newspaper.

I want to hear something else.

CHARITY. I read the rest of it last night

When we got home.

MOTHER. At five in the morning?!

CHARITY. Yes. I've wanted to read it since I was fourteen.

> (**CHARITY** *walks to the bag, gets the newspaper out, and hands it to* **MOTHER**.)

MOTHER. No reading for me.

My eyes.

But I'll listen.

CHARITY. *(Excited.)* Okay.

Let me get you the funny news from December of 1828.

There was a very comical short dialogue in here.

About

Like a tragedy

An enslaved person

Comes to bring his young master at college bad news.

And instead of telling him the worst of the worst news first

He tells the smallest of the worst news first

And then the master is kind of relieved

But the slave

Keeps going

And keeps going

It's starts with a crow dying

But it ends with all his family dead.

MOTHER. "Charity!" Why did you tell me what it was about?

You've spoiled it for me.

CHARITY. Wait.

No.

There's other stuff.

MOTHER. But I know the ending.

Never give away the ending Charity.

> *(Other graves we didn't know were graves that glow a different green [the green of the National Flag of Sierra Leone] in the grass.)*

The wind feels different.

CHARITY. I don't see anyone.

MOTHER. I pay attention to the hints nature provides us.

How the **wind feels,** and the **trees move**.

The beat of the soil.

Its way of holding our weight.

You must be sensitive to the shifts.

> *(A Black man approaches. It is the **JANITOR** (**CUFFEE**).)*

JANITOR. Evenin'.

MOTHER. Evenin'.

JANITOR. You both should be inside

It's

Three in the morning.

Aren't you cold?

MOTHER. Yes.

Though, it's a warmer October than last October.

1831 was a colder year.

More rain than this year too.

Philadelphia is getting warmer perhaps.

Who would know – Who would know?

.

How is the world treatin' you this evening?

JANITOR. Well, I began my shift a bit of an hour ago at the medical college.

MOTHER. Jefferson?

JANITOR. That is the one.

MOTHER. Are you married?

JANITOR. …

MOTHER. *(With a coldness.)* I ask because it must be hard

To have to sleep

With your husband away

Working.

JANITOR. *(Defensive.)* I have a wife, yes.

And a young son.

MOTHER. I've never seen you around

Are you from Moyamensing?

I never go that way.

JANITOR. No. I live at the Medical college.

I am their janitor.

MOTHER. I see.

JANITOR. John Petersburg had me arrive this evening, in his stead.

It took me a long while to arrive

I've never been to this church

But John he said it was of *grave* impor/

Ha.

Sorry.

He said he was in dire

It's a

My apologies.

There's a need for this body

since it's paid for.

MOTHER. How can it be paid for when he's no longer living?

JANITOR. *(Approaches.)* Here is the paper mam.

MOTHER. *(Hands the paper to* **CHARITY**.*)* Charity?

CHARITY. *(Takes the note and reads.)* This is just a note.

A note of agreement.

It says dad was Henry Petersburg's employee.

And to hand the cadaver over to John Petersburg.

This is just a note.

This is nothing.

No is our answer.

MOTHER. *(Nodding no.)* Charity. *(To* **JANITOR**.*)* We could go to court for this.

JANITOR. Henry sent a letter to John, his brother, about the circumstance of his driver, a Black man called Moses, who took ill in New York.

Henry was at a loss of funds from gambling the night before.

And owed more than he possessed.

He messaged his brother with the details of your husband's illness knowing it would be of interest because John is a student at the Medical college.

So, there was an exchange.

John sent for his brother

And your husband's safe return to Philadelphia.

With the understanding your husband was on his last hours before the Cholera would take him.

MOTHER. I've never known a lifeless body to be wagered on!

JANITOR. You are brave.

This is my first time

Witnessing an individual present at this hour

Let alone a Black woman and her daughter

I wonder what led you here.

How you knew to come?

MOTHER. My mind haunted me the morning we had Moses' private burial.

The thoughts came in stronger as the early evening came.

"Protect Moses"

"Guard Moses"

"Stay Close"

The urge to protect my husband.

A primal urge.

> *(Intensely direct.)*

There are rumors about your kind.

I decided to see for myself.

I didn't want to believe it.

My daughter said she felt this same urge.

But it spoke to her differently.

"Stay with mom"

"Stay close to mom"

But now the thought I can't shake is

<u>"How can you, a Black man, how can you live with yourself?"</u>

JANITOR. It's for science.

We do it

To advance science.

CHARITY. Do you believe in god?

JANITOR. I do not.

CHARITY. My daddy's' spirit is on its way to African heaven. It takes time.

JANITOR. His spirit?

MOTHER. Yes. He has distant family from Bunce Island in Sierra Leone.

JANITOR. I am here with a timed deadline.

To do a job.

Decomposing bodies are rendered unusable after seventy-two hours.

I cannot give you the time you desire.

(Attempting a cold kindness.)

If in your world, an afterlife exists

He's there already

Give it a break.

MOTHER. Why do you get to decide that?

JANITOR. We put the bones back.

I bury the bones.

BACK.

After preparation and dissection.

He'll get there.

OK?

MOTHER. I've never seen you around town.

It must be easy to make such big decisions, while mollycoddled under dastardly white people.

JANITOR. Mam.

MOTHER. I could go to the cops.

They'd throw you in jail for being a resurrectionist.

JANITOR. *(This is his identity.)* When the 20th or 21st century gets here

There will be no more deaths due to Cholera

Or Tuberculosis

The Fevers

None of it.

Because of what we're doing now.

This October only one person has fallen ill to Cholera.

Which is why this body carries great meaning to the Medical school.

And even more so to John.

He was the first to discover Cholera's link to water.

And you understand <u>now</u> the importance to heat your water in order to clean it!

The advancements John continues to make can change the world.

His findings have already been published.

And has led to a flood of donations to continue this research.

MOTHER. *(Referring to herself and* CHARITY.*)* His research is for the benefit of white people, not us.

If John does create some sort of medicine to treat Cholera.

I would not receive treatment, nor my daughter if we needed it.

It would remain as White people medicine to go on White people shelves.

As they are who everything goes to first.

So why should I sacrifice my husband's body, for medicine he/me/or my child wouldn't receive?

JANITOR. How do you know that?!

MOTHER. Just look at the outbreak that happened during the summer.

Black people helped White people, we became bleeders, nurses, grave diggers because White people convinced us that we weren't susceptible to getting it.

Then Black people got Cholera.

Who was there to help us?

No one.

Henry let my husband die.

JANITOR. ...

MOTHER. What's going to happen to your body?! You made a deal with the devil?

JANITOR. I will be buried on campus

My son will succeed me in my practice and will ensure no harm

I mean

No robbing

MOTHER. Harm.

You were right.

IF you wouldn't want your own body to

To be paid for

Or stolen

Without your knowledge.

Why would you allow it to happen to others?

JANITOR. This practice will not cease.

Bodies are needed for training.

So, medical students can operate

So, they can study the body and help prevent illnesses

To treat the ill

It's a good practice.

MOTHER. I know you all take from the jails

And hospitals

The almshouses

And/

I am going to show you something.

> *(Takes out ten dollars.)*

How much did he pay you for this job?

JANITOR. Three dollars. I'm doing this job as a favor.

MOTHER. I live at Pine Street.

Charity attends the African School for the Youth on Race Street right near the park.

I'm a business owner.

I've saved everything I've ever made

If you'd like ten extra dollars.

It's yours

You take it

On this condition.

You will lie to John.

You will say.

> *(Making it up.)*

Tonight, while on your way to the church to resurrect Moses' body you fell ill

With severe stomach cramps

And had to return home

You thought it may be Cholera.

But it was spoiled milk.

JANITOR. And if he requires me to return tomorrow evening?

MOTHER. John will need to ensure the body comes back.

On the third day.

He'll return himself.

JANITOR. Okay.

Okay.

>   (**JANITOR** *puts his hand out.*)

MOTHER. Five for now.

Five for later.

JANITOR. When?

MOTHER. I'm good for it.

You know where I live.

Where Charity attends school.

This is our church.

Come find me.

>   (**JANITOR** *exits.*)

CHARITY. …

MOTHER. A dream without a plan is just a wish.

CHARITY. *(Throws up water.)*

>   *(Mid throw up.)*

You didn't prepare me for this night.

MOTHER. Nor did I prepare myself.

(They sit. A violin plays a song reminiscent of "Lift Every Voice And Sing" mixed with a current new Hip Hop song*, we can't fully tell what it is. They lie down. They stand. They sit.)

(They lie down. They stand. They are speaking to one another inaudibly. Dawn approaches. They walk towards the exit. The clock dings. They see 17:00:00 hours. They stop/look at the clock and exit.)

---

* A licence to produce *The Great Privation* does not include a performance licence for any third-party or copyrighted music. Licensees should create an original composition or use music in the public domain. For further information, please see the Music and Third-Party Materials Use Note on page iii.

Scene Four

(It is present day. Mid-afternoon. **JOHN** *enters followed by* **MOTHER** *and* **CHARITY**. *They are all carrying their lunch trays.)*

JOHN. *(In mid conversation.)* The song keeps playing in my head.

MOTHER. I know.

JOHN. Why'd we never learn that song here at training?

MOTHER. The Harlem Camp Lightford is pretty lit.

CHARITY. I went there as a kid.

JOHN. Yeah.

It's like

We only do "baby shark" here.

And they're

Mature kids

They don't even like "F" *(F***.)* with that show.

CHARITY. I know.

JOHN. *(Singing at a lower voice.)* You can't ride my little red wagon.

CHARITY.	**MOTHER**.
You can't ride my little red wagon.	You can't ride my little red wagon.

JOHN. The wheels are busted, and the ASS is dragging.

CHARITY & MOTHER. *(Correcting him because he remixed the song.)* The wheels are busted and the AXELS draggin'.

JOHN. CHUG CHUG second verse.

CHARITY & MOTHER. CHUG CHUG second verse.

JOHN. A little bit louder, a little bit WORSE.

CHARITY & MOTHER. A LITTLE LOUDER A LITTLE BIT WORSE.

CHARITY. YOU CAN'T RIDE MY LITTLE RED WAGON

JOHN & MOTHER. YOU CAN'T RIDE MY LITTLE RED WAGON

CHARITY. THE WHEELS ARE BUSTED AND THE *(Twerks.)* ASS IS DRAGGIN'.

JOHN & MOTHER. THE WHEELS ARE BUSTED AND THE *(Twerks.)* ASS IS DRAGGIN'.

CHARITY. CHUG CHUG THIRD VERSE.

JOHN & MOTHER.. CHUG CHUG THIRD VERSE.

CHARITY. ALITTLE bit louder a little bit worse.

JOHN.	**MOTHER.**
A little bit louder a little bit worse.	*(Shocked.)* **A little bit louder a little bit worse**.

MOTHER. *(Dancing real "hood like".)* YOU CAN'T RIDE MY LITTLE RED WAGON.

CHARITY & JOHN. YOU CAN'T RIDE MY LITTLE RED WAGON.

MOTHER. THE WHEELS ARE BUSTED.

    *(**CUFFEE** bursts in.)*

CUFFEE. *(Awkward and positive simultaneously.)* Hello.

Hello.

Hi,

I know you're on break.

Please

Keep it down

Other campers are still in session

I'm glad you're having fun.

.

.

.

Okay.

CHARITY & MOTHER. Sorry.

> (**CUFFEE** *smiles & exits.*)

JOHN. (**JOHN** *gives middle fingers, pretends to fight, and possibly pretends to eat* **CUFFEE** *and shit him out.*) **FFFFFFFFFFFFFFF you.**

Your STAFF

Are having fun on their LUNCH BREAK.

A small break from these nasty ass kids.

Are we drinking?

Are we smoking on the job?

LIKE YOUR OTHER STAFF?

No

We're the good staff

Singing a children's song for two seconds and YOU WANNA COME IN

AND RUIN It????

What a leech.

> (**CUFFEE** *enters, smiles, and makes a cup of coffee from the already heated pot and exits.*)

Ew.

CHARITY. You feel strongly.

JOHN. Cuffee would sleep *while* we were teaching the campers.

CHARITY.	**MOTHER**.
Are you serious?	Wow.

JOHN. And I never told on him or anything.

CHARITY. He fell asleep?

JOHN. He was in a period of fasting, I think.

I don't know for Ramadan?

I don't know

But he would doze off

All the time

Even while standing.

CHARITY. Oh. Wow.

JOHN. And like

I'm just

I just feel like I should've gotten the promotion.

Cuffee worked one summer here.

I've worked three.

I know I have a strong personality

But I can be the camp supervisor.

I am capable.

And now

He gets thirty an hour.

CHARITY.	**MOTHER**.
WHAT?	WHAT?

JOHN. For doing nothing.

 Besides watching us.

 And listening to kids like Timmy complain.

CHARITY. Oh.

JOHN. And now you understand why I hate him.

> (**CUFFEE** *enters, smiles, gets rice milk from the locked staff fridge, pours it in his coffee, and exits.*)

(Woe is me.) I get twenty-two an hour/

CHARITY.	**MOTHER**.
Twenty-two?!	Twenty-two?!

JOHN. Yeah.

 It's ridiculous.

CHARITY.	**MOTHER**.
… *(Mouths "wow.")*	…

> *(They begin to eat in silence for a second.)*

JOHN. I feel like I'd have so much fun at the Harlem Camp Lightford.

MOTHER. *(Just going along with it.)* Oh yeah, for sure.

JOHN. I just would love to go to Harlem.

 Even live there.

 It must be so nice.

MOTHER. It is.

JOHN. Why did you leave?

MOTHER. We're here for the summer.

 My mom requested to live here

 For her final months.

She was born in Philadelphia

Moved to Harlem when she was ten.

We're all living with my great aunt.

JOHN. Oh. I'm so sorry.

MOTHER. We don't know Phili at all.

I'm still not entirely sure why she wanted to come.

Her and my great aunt weren't very close to my knowledge.

But we helped her make this trip.

Kidney Failure.

The Dialysis gave her eight years, but it doesn't seem like she has much longer.

JOHN. …

MOTHER. And I told Camp Lightford about my situation in the city.

They connected me to this Philly location.

I said I would like to keep my daughter close to me in this new city because she's all of a sudden decided she was pro-Black and pro-vandalism of school property.

> (**JOHN***'s like, "What's pro-Black".* **CHARITY** *is like "ha-ha mom".)*

And they helped.

> (**MOTHER** *gives* **CHARITY** *a stop fake laughing look.)*

But, not that much, considering, me and my daughter make seven dollars less than you.

JOHN. I've been here for three summers.

That's probably how it works.

MOTHER. I've worked at the New York City branch for five. And I have a child and mother to provide for.

JOHN. Oh. I see.

MOTHER. Same here.

CHARITY. *(Contextualizing it for* **JOHN**.*)* My school was built in 1951. There was a faint "Colored only" etching over this water fountain that doesn't even work anymore. I spray painted it with a Black power fist. And I went viral cuz my friends recorded me. Mom's a hater.

> *(***JOHN*** makes a "Yikes. I don't know how to respond to that" face.)*

MOTHER. *(Speed of lightning and not said seriously.)* Oh, so I'm a hater because I want you to get into college and be the first in our family to pursue higher learning?

CHARITY. The right colleges will vibe with my video.

MOTHER. Vibe. Vibe. Okay. Maybe MY VIBES ARE OFF. I'm just a vibeless bore. And I should just hang loose.

CHARITY. Sans-vibes yes. Hang loose ma, **you're lacking "rizz"**.

MOTHER. *("What is Rizz?")* Rizz?

JOHN. *(Saying it super loud almost insensitively for* **MOTHER** *with a smile.)* Ca-RIZZ-Ma. *(Charisma.)*

MOTHER. Did Nashelle or Jamir- did either one of them participate? Nope. But you decided it was alright. WHY'D THAT "LIGHTLY ETCHED COLOREDS ONLY" SIGN **JUST** START BOTHERING YOU-HUH?! YOU'VE BEEN AT THAT SCHOOL FOR THREE YEARS NOW.

CHARITY. You know, mom! There are three Black kids in my school including me cuz you sent me to school FAR from where we live which fine, I get it, fine right?

Nashelle's great great grandma wrote books. Nashelle's grandma worked with Angela Davis. Nashelle's mom has a non-profit bringing affordable- sustainable salad bars to Harlem. Jamir's dad organized twenty BLM demonstrations in NYC. What about us? What about our family? Nashelle and Jamir just rave and rave about how their college essays are going to be better than mine. I have nothing to show for! And Jamir said, we need to make each Black generation who comes AFTER us more liberated than we are **NOW so I earned my Black stripes**. And and, I have to say John. Mom was on my side, till she found out about the video. She's just worried about nothing!

MOTHER. All I'm saying is-is-just cuz-just cuz Nashelle and Jamir's family got famous people doing activism things, don't mean we aint have nothing to show for. And I'll have you know, by just surviving we're making the world a better place.

CHARITY. **I want more.** I want to know MORE about US. I'm sure. All the women in our family lineage are strong, independent women! They've done something-some activism! I don't care if it's small or if it was big, I just want to know.

MOTHER. So your grandma being a school nurse wasn't impressive enough? Your Dad, being a safety agent at New York Elementary for ten years before he passed-not deep enough? Me taking care of children? Do I not reach your standards?

CHARITY. *(Fuming with emotion.)* You're not listening! **On your side of the family ma.** BEFORE grandma. Before great grandma. I want to know where we come from. Who's on the top of our family tree? I won't ever know Daddy's side, you don't know them like that, I certainly don't know them, but we're sitting on an opportunity to know MORE, and it bothers me that you don't CARE.

MOTHER. What if we were just people daughter? You want a talented tenth family to rave about?

CHARITY. Your gaslighting me.

> (**MOTHER**'s *eyes bulge wide open.*)

MOTHER. We're pausing the conversation. It's done. You're saying young people terms that feel made up and it's giving me a headache. Stop.

CHARITY. This is what happens when you talk to Millennials. Every time!

MOTHER. Enough.

> (**CHARITY** *and* **MOTHER** *look at* **JOHN**. **JOHN** *has his mouth open from shock and sits up stiffly.*)
>
> (*He looks at* **MOTHER**. *He looks at* **CHARITY**.)
>
> (*He looks to the ceiling.*)

JOHN. *(Changing the subject quite quickly.)* UM. UM. UM. Have you seen the grounds out back at night?

MOTHER.	**CHARITY**.
No.	No.

MOTHER. *(Continued.)* We head to my great aunt's house after work ends.

JOHN. I didn't put that together.

You **don't** sleep here, like us.

MOTHER. They made an exception for our situation.

JOHN. But, at night, like there's some trippy ISH.

CHARITY. Trippy?

JOHN. Yeah.

MOTHER. How so?

JOHN. This mess hall was 100% built in front of a graveyard, from the early 19th century.

CHARITY. NO?

JOHN. Before this was a mess hall, it was a CHURCH.

CHARITY. I think graveyards are cool!

JOHN. *(Stands up and points to a front window.)* It's right behind us.

If Cuffee was doing his job

> *(**CUFFEE** enters.)*

He would've remembered to say that at training.

I'll show you tonight if you hang around late.

> *(**CUFFEE** unlocks the staff refrigerator loudly, retrieves his lunch, and slowly walks to the exit.)*

CUFFEE. *(Because he's heard all of **JOHN**'s trash talking.)* John.

Make sure the door is closed on staff breaks.

> *(**CUFFEE** walks towards the exit and looks back at **JOHN**.)*

JOHN. Got it.

> *(Everyone freezes.)*

> *(**CUFFEE** makes an announcement.)*

CUFFEE. *(Offstage.)* Group 2.

Lunchtime is over.

Counselors, please head over to the cafeteria to pick up your campers.

Repeating Counselors please head over to the cafeteria to pick up your campers.

Happy International Plastic Bag Free Day!

JOHN. *(Screams in anxious panic.)* Why is that a holiday?!

CHARITY. You never know with Cuffee.

Let's just give him the permission to be different.

JOHN. I'll shut up I guess.

> *(All clean up their things and walk towards the exit.)*

CHARITY. Mom? Could we stay here tonight?

I'd like to see the gravesite.

MOTHER. Charity

We don't do that.

White people do that.

CHARITY. We can pray before

Like for god to protect us.

Please.

Please.

Come on.

You literally separated me from my friends for an entire summer.

You took my phone.

Grandma and Auntie only watch soap operas all day.

I'm suffering.

This is the only thing I actually want to do.

Please.

MOTHER. I'll think about it.

CHARITY. YAY.

MOTHER. I didn't say yes.

CHARITY. Ugh. Fine.

(They exit.)

(The dirt underneath the separate graves pop up like popcorn and land in their respective spots as if nothing happened. Then the sound of live African drums, play a song [a song played at funerals] and the grave's dirt pops up and dances along with the music.)*

* A licence to produce *The Great Privation* does not include a performance licence for any third-party or copyrighted recordings. Licensees should create their own.

Scene Five

(It is October 23rd, 1832. It is one in the morning. The lights are darker than last time. Dread fills the space with the sound of wind.)

MOTHER. You can never get used to the night.

CHARITY. What scares me are the eyes that are watching me.

The ones I can't see.

MOTHER. I hear everything.

The wind

The leaves traveling

The animals finding their resting spots

The children being tucked into bed by their parents.

(Starts tearing up.)

I haven't been able to do that for you.

Not lately.

And I'm sorry for it.

CHARITY. May I sleep in bed with you tonight?

MOTHER. Yes, Charity.

CHARITY. I'm thinking that I should become a teacher.

And teach adults how to read in night school.

What do you think?

MOTHER. That sounds amazing.

CHARITY. I just would need to practice.

Maybe with someone who needs it first.

Before I go and ask to apprentice under a teacher.

MOTHER. Yes. Of course.

CHARITY. ...

MOTHER. *(Feeling vulnerable.)* Well. My sweet Charity.

We have something in common.

I've always wanted to read the paper.

But, I've never known how.

CHARITY. Okay Mommie.

> *(**CHARITY** retrieves the paper and a letter and sits next to her **MOTHER**.)*

I wanted to make sure Daddy was around to hear it.

MOTHER. What?

CHARITY. Today in English class

Our teacher said to write a letter to the person they'd like to be like

A hero

Or somebody.

And I wrote something.

May I read it?

> *(**CHARITY** sits next to her **MOTHER**, and points as she reads.)*

Hi Missy Freeman. That's you!

MOTHER. That's me!

CHARITY. *(Continues reading.)* I have been a tricky daughter, haven't I?

I have made it seem at times that your advice carries no serious consideration in my mind.

Your strength has scared me.

Shaken me to my core.

Because it's beyond what I've ever seen on earth.

Oops. Wait Mommy. That's not how earth is supposed to be spelled. It's e-a-r-t-h. Not e-r-a-t-h.

MOTHER. Okay.

CHARITY. You and I are different.

And we are the same.

You get mad at me because I'm stubborn

But you laugh, because my angry faces

Were once yours.

Without the wrinkles.

MOTHER. I don't have wrinkles Charity!

CHARITY. Let me finish!

I love every bit of who you are

I will never stop loving you

Since you are my first "I love you".

MOTHER. Goodness Charity.

CHARITY. You see!

MOTHER. Thank you.

CHARITY. I love you.

MOTHER. That was very sweet.

For some reason I thought the letter was to your father.

CHARITY. No. I love Dad.

But, you're my hero.

Dad can be my second hero.

MOTHER. I told him not to take Henry to New York.

Because of the outbreak in the city.

I warned him.

He still went.

CHARITY. Daddy's stubborn.

MOTHER. I know.

He always was.

Okay teach me more.

From the newspaper.

> (**CHARITY** *grabs the newspaper, sits next to* **MOTHER**, *and reads, in sotto voice. Two flashlights land on the frames of* **CHARITY** *and* **MOTHER**'s *bodies and movements. We are scared at first. A third light appears it's* **JOHN**.)

JOHN (MODERN DAY). *(With flashlights.)* Sh! Sh!

> *(When Modern Day* **JOHN** *enters. In his own world. He is oblivious that two ghosts from 1832 are visibly present, both ghosts onstage take over the voices and bodies of Modern Day* **CHARITY** *and* **MOTHER**. **JOHN** *is strictly in White People LA LA Land. The old and the new merge. Who is who?)*

CHARITY (MODERN DAY). What time is it?

MOTHER (MODERN DAY). One a.m. What if we get caught?

JOHN (MODERN DAY). We won't!

We're allowed to be on the property.

We're the adults.

Well not you Charity.

CHARITY (MODERN DAY). I'm sixteen.

JOHN (MODERN DAY). Come, come, slowly.

(***Sound of an owl.*** *All look up.*)

CHARITY (MODERN DAY). What the...?

JOHN (MODERN DAY). It's an owl.

MOTHER (MODERN DAY). We can leave Charity.

CHARITY (MODERN DAY). No. I'd like to look around.

It doesn't look like a gravesite to me.

JOHN (MODERN DAY). That's what the developers thought too.

MOTHER (MODERN DAY). And how do you know?

JOHN (MODERN DAY). ...

MOTHER (MODERN DAY). I feel off. Really off.

JOHN (MODERN DAY). It's a strange feeling here.

(*Flashlight on* **CHARITY**.)

I like your coat.

CHARITY (MODERN DAY). It was my dad's.

JOHN (MODERN DAY). Oh, he's/

MOTHER (MODERN DAY). /We lost him earlier this year.

JOHN (MODERN DAY). Oh, my goodness.

I'm so sorry.

How did he die?

MOTHER (MODERN DAY). ...

JOHN. You don't have to say how.

I lost my dad at sixteen because of a blood clot.

CHARITY (MODERN DAY). Oh.

      *(**CHARITY** shows **JOHN** a picture of her dad*
      in a locket.)

This is him.

He is "too fine" to be laid up in someone's hospital bed,
he'd say.

      *(**MOTHER** steps closer to **CHARITY**.)*

*(**CHARITY** is teary eyed.)* My dad was great.

JOHN (MODERN DAY). Look,

If you ever need to talk.

Or

Someone to cry with, I'm here.

      *(**JOHN** steps onto Moses' grave. The dirt pops*
      *up. It glows and transforms **JOHN** to 1832 [a*
      *possession almost], which then has **MOTHER***
      *and **CHARITY** see that the **JOHN** from the*
      past is in the room.)

JOHN (1832). Good evening ladies.

CHARITY & MOTHER (1832). Good evening.

JOHN (1832). I am in a rush.

CHARITY (1832). Aren't we all?

JOHN (1832). I want to say.

The body currently in that pine box.

Is no longer your father.

An alive man.

No longer a driver for my brother.

He is a body.

His soul is with Jesus in heaven.

MOTHER (1832). You should've looked for another body by now.

JOHN (1832). I've put much money forth for this one.

> (**MOTHER** *puts thirty dollars on the floor.*)

MOTHER (1832). *(Furious and devastated to put money forth for her husband's corpse.)* I never thought in my life

That my husband's body

Held some sort of price after death!

JOHN (1832). …

MOTHER (1832). *(Crying.)* You people.

You Doctors.

If this is what you do to become a doctor

I will never see one of you for as long as I live!

JOHN (1832). Well, your kind avoid hospitals.

MOTHER (1832). And you can understand why, can't you?

JOHN (1832). Sure.

MOTHER (1832). Will you take this money?

> (**MOTHER** *and* **JOHN** *have a standoff in regard to who picks up the money.* **JOHN** *picks up the money, and puts his hand out for more.*)

JOHN (1832). Thirty-five would suffice. That's enough for the trouble you've cost me.

MOTHER (1832). Thirty-five it is.

> (**MOTHER** *digs for money, and gestures to hand* **JOHN** *money.*)

CHARITY (1832). HAND HIM NO MORE MOTHER. Leave monster! Get away from my family.

JOHN (1832). **You'll never see me again, nor I you.**

> (**JOHN** *pushes his hand out more violently.* **MOTHER** *hands* **JOHN** *five more dollars, by* **MOTHER** *and* **JOHN** *touching, they are thrust into their modern-day descendants.*)

MOTHER (MODERN DAY). *(Touching her chest.)* I feel trouble.

I feel the weight of time in this space.

CHARITY (MODERN DAY). *(Grabbing her stomach.)* I feel violence.

I feel the weight of time in this space.

MOTHER (MODERN DAY). John, do you feel it?

> (**JOHN** *looks at the two lights behind him. He goes closer to it, walks backwards, and then looks at* **CHARITY** *and* **MOTHER**. *He is confused. He now is addressing the* **CHARITY** *and* **MOTHER** *as if they are the* **CHARITY** *and* **MOTHER** *he believes is from the present day.*)

JOHN (MODERN DAY). *(Grabs one side of his face/brain and feels compelled/forced into speaking.)* I have some freaky stuff in our family home.

There's been a box in my family for generations.

That I was banned from opening.

MOTHER (MODERN DAY). Okay.

JOHN (MODERN DAY). You know.

Descendants from bad people

Bad old "Americans"

Can have some freaky heirlooms passed down.

Usually, the guilty family members of future generations dispose of or bury those items with said family member.

Especially white American's *(Whispers.)* "from the south".

You could only imagine.

MOTHER (MODERN DAY). I don't have heirlooms.

JOHN (MODERN DAY). Well not always an heirloom.

Notes.

Bills.

Diaries.

Death Masks.

Newspapers.

Those items.

CHARITY (MODERN DAY). And you have those?

JOHN (MODERN DAY). Yes.

And since we've started camp this summer, I get these whispers from here *(Referring to the area surrounding Moses' grave.)*

At night.

It's a woman's voice. Maybe two.

They tell me to "Open the box".

      *(***CHARITY*** and ***MOTHER*** look at one another.)*

Since I was little, I've wanted to.

      *(***CHARITY*** and ***MOTHER*** look at ***JOHN*** like, "That's a strange thing to say".)*

CHARITY (MODERN DAY). …

JOHN. ...

> (**JOHN** *begins walking towards the exit staring down* **CHARITY** *and* **MOTHER**.)

CHARITY (MODERN DAY). Where are you going?

> (**JOHN** *begins backing up slowly.* **CHARITY** *and* **MOTHER** *back up towards the two flashlights held beaming upstage. They grab hold of them and quickly enter. Time warps forward for* **CHARITY** *and* **MOTHER***, and not for* **JOHN**.)

John! Sorry we took longer than we meant to! Mom took forever to convince!

MOTHER (MODERN DAY). John?

JOHN (MODERN DAY). (**AS MODERN JOHN.**) I don't –

> (**JOHN** *is experiencing a possession.*)

(*As other* **JOHN (1832)**.) For tonight.

I will do as you wish.

(*As* **MOTHER (1832)**.) The journey to Africa takes around three days.

(*As* **JOHN (1832**.) Shorten it.

> (**JOHN** *exits, frightened.*)

MOTHER (MODERN DAY). I know he said his Cancer sign was in Saturn tonight.

I don't know what that means.

John is off.

He looked at us like we were ghosts!

CHARITY (MODERN DAY). Should we go after him?

MOTHER (MODERN DAY). Never go after a white man in a graveyard.

> *(The sounds of cheers fill the air. We don't know where they're coming from. We hear dancing and happy screaming. The "ghosts" of 1832 have been able to scare **JOHN**'s descendant off for the final time.)*

I feel something.

> *(They look around.)*

CHARITY (MODERN DAY). My heart is racing.

MOTHER (MODERN DAY). Mine too.

It's incredible, this feeling.

Thrilling.

> *(They look up. They both kneel on opposite sides of Moses' grave and touch the soil. It glows. They have a rush of new language and memories from their ancestors.)*

Scene Six

(It is a scene blended in with the one before.)

CHARITY (1832). I didn't bring any food with me tonight.

MOTHER (1832). And whose fault is that?

CHARITY (1832). Mine.

MOTHER (1832). I told you to pack a snack. Didn't I?

CHARITY (1832). Yes. Mom. Why do you have to do *the I told you so* tonight? We should be celebrating!

MOTHER (1832). I'm not happy Charity.

Why would you think I was?

CHARITY (1832). Because we got rid of the resurrectionist!

MOTHER (1832). I am not okay.

I've been shaking for three days.

CHARITY (1832). Faith told me that God is white. Think it's true?

MOTHER (1832). Faith is full of it.

CHARITY (1832). You don't believe that?

MOTHER (1832). No, I don't believe that.

CHARITY (1832). It's a full moon tonight.

MOTHER (1832). Yes, it is.

CHARITY (1832). **Can we play cards?**

MOTHER (1832). No.

CHARITY (1832). Can we dance?

MOTHER (1832). There's no music.

CHARITY (1832). Can we sing?

MOTHER (1832). It's too late.

CHARITY (1832). How long do we have to stay here? We've won!

MOTHER (1832). Charity. Please.

Take a nap.

Close your eyes.

CHARITY (1832). Oh Mom.

I want to be in my bed.

MOTHER (1832). Give it some time.

CHARITY (1832). I'm cold.

MOTHER (1832). Me too.

CHARITY (1832). I'm hungry.

MOTHER (1832). Your being hungry has made me hungry now.

CHARITY (1832). I'm sad as well. Like you.

MOTHER (1832). Alright.

CHARITY (1832). Angry that we must be here still.

MOTHER (1832). Okay.

CHARITY (1832). *(New teenage thought.)* What's intercourse like?

MOTHER (1832). WHAT?!

CHARITY (1832). I've never had it. MOM come ON. TELL ME.

MOTHER (1832). No. Not tonight. No.

(We are continually in 1832.)

CHARITY. There's nothing to DO out here!

MOTHER. Can we play the seeing game?

CHARITY. You can't see far enough to play that game.

MOTHER. I'm thinking of a number between one to ten.

CHARITY. You think up the drabbest of games.

MOTHER. …

    (**CHARITY** *sits on the other side of the tree.*)

Charity, how was school today?

CHARITY. It was fine.

MOTHER. You wrote that nice letter.

    (New thought.)

Stinky, are you looking forward to church on Sunday?

CHARITY. No, because the guard is a traitor.

MOTHER. Sure.

I can get behind that.

    (Trying to entertain her daughter.)

Stunk butt, are you excited for your last year of school?

CHARITY. No, I like school. *(New thought.)* Mother, I feel like you always have it together. Are you ever not perfect?

MOTHER. Look at where we are.

I'm serious.

Look.

Does this

Us being here.

In any way prove me to be perfect or good?

CHARITY. I think you're perfect.

MOTHER. You haven't seen the way I look in the morning then.

It's far from that.

CHARITY. You are done up before I wake up. You need to let loose.

MOTHER. Let loose?

CHARITY. Yah.

Hang loose Ma.

MOTHER. That isn't English.

CHARITY. Let your hair blow in the wind.

Shake out those coils.

> (**MOTHER** *does so.*)

Oh. Are we about this?

> (**CHARITY** *takes her hair out of her ponytail. They shake their hair in unison.* **CHARITY** *makes a mustache with her mom's hair, which shows* **MOTHER***'s hair shrinkage. Upon releasing her mom's coils,* **MOTHER***'s hair springs back to her scalp quite quickly.*)

MOTHER. I've hung loose.

> (**CHARITY** *hugs her* **MOTHER.**)

Get our things.

CHARITY. We're leaving?

MOTHER. (*A Black mom's way of saying this.*) COME here.

CHARITY. (*Does so.*) Yes?

MOTHER. (*Touching her hair.*) When's the last time you've combed your hair?

Oh my god.

Are there rings around your neck?

Do you wash your neck?

Charity?!

Charity?!

CHARITY. Mother!

Can you not be a Mom for a second?

MOTHER. Fine.

> (**MOTHER** *starts walking towards the exit.*)

CHARITY. It hurts to comb my hair.

The comb is violent and takes out too much.

MOTHER. Have you been putting the grease from root to end like I've told you to, BEFORE you use the comb?

CHARITY. (*Catching up behind her* **MOTHER**.) ...

MOTHER. Have you?

Umhum.

CHARITY. Wait.

> (**CHARITY** *and* **MOTHER** *turn around.*
> **CHARITY** *looks at the grave. She's strong and
> weak.*)

We miss you Dad.

You are smart.

You had such a wonderful laugh.

I like that you inhaled your food and made a mess at the table after meals.

I miss hearing your feet move around in the kitchen late at night, because that's when I could finally get to sleep, when I knew you were homc.

And I miss you making fun of me.

And your man hair on the tile floor in the bathroom.

I miss when you'd dance with me, mommy can't dance.

Who will dance with me now?

It feels like half of my heart is gone.

MOTHER. How can that be when half of him is you?

> (**MOTHER** *offers her hand with a bow.*
> **MOTHER** *and* **CHARITY** *try to dance, a
> dance that shows us two young women who
> absolutely love each other. The dancing takes
> them offstage. There's a moment of stillness.*)

> (*The stage turns red. The clock glows
> at, -4:00:00.* **JOHN** *re-enters with all of the
> materials that would haunt us. We see* **JOHN**
> *dig. We see* **JOHN** *jump into the grave with
> the claw and burlap bag. We see* **JOHN** *use the
> claw. We don't see* **JOHN** *put the body in the
> bag since he is in the grave.* **JOHN** *jumps out
> of the grave, and drags the body up.* **JOHN**
> *places the dirt back into the grave, and drags
> the body offstage. The stage is empty.*)

Scene Seven

(It is present day. Mid-afternoon. It is July 4th. **CHARITY** *and* **MOTHER** *enter the cabin with their lunch treys.)*

MOTHER. Do you have a favorite camper?

CHARITY. Not one. I like the ones who misbehave. Who knows why!

MOTHER. I like Imani.

She was like you when you were little.

CHARITY. I knew you would say that.

MOTHER. Has big eyes like yours.

CHARITY. Sure...

MOTHER. Sensitive too.

CHARITY. We're at work.

> *(***MOTHER***'s phone buzzes.)*

Oh.

> *(***MOTHER*** *looks at her phone, smiles, and instantly puts her phone away.* ***CHARITY*** *glances.)*

Who was that?

MOTHER. Not important.

CHARITY. Who is Jermaine?!

MOTHER. No one. No one. Nothing.

Don't concern yourself with grown folk's business.

> *(***CHARITY*** *squints her eyes.* ***MOTHER*** *squints back.* ***MOTHER*** *giggles.)*

CHARITY. Uh-huh. Anywho. Why we're you written up twice?

MOTHER. It was before you attended the camp that one summer.

It was for Group 3.

The eleven-year-olds.

A kid named Dwayne was playing basketball during free time and bit his tongue open while trying to shoot.

Blood was gushing everywhere.

You know I hate blood.

I left the room.

CHARITY. YOU LEFT ALL OF THE KIDS IN THE ROOM?

MOTHER. Well.

Crystal was in the room.

Tatiana was on break.

MOTHER. Crystal handled it but told on me in the incident report.

She's a snitch.

The second write up was after a trip to the Bronx Zoo

My group lost a kid.

CHARITY. HUH?

MOTHER. Same year.

Terrible times.

I was in charge of the headcount on the school bus heading back to Harlem.

I miscounted.

Zeek was a quiet kid.

It's STRESSFUL having to go on a trip anywhere with children.

You go in and out of these dark rooms with these short ass kids

That look just like the animals on display.

CHARITY. Oh my god.

MOTHER. Our group saw that animal movie with the Dolphins at the zoo.

We went on the trolley.

We had to eat in the cafeteria.

WITH all the other camps they had in their facilities that day.

And

And

I mean luckily all of our kids had the camp shirt on.

It was EASIER to not lose them.

But

We get back to Harlem

And get a call from the Bronx Zoo.

Zeek was fine

He cried but he was fine.

He got locked in a bathroom stall.

But he was fine.

CHARITY. Oh my god.

MOTHER. I don't know how

But

My whole team including Crystal got written up.

Which is why I still can't afford to get you a nice laptop for school.

CHARITY. I'll chip in.

I can only use the computers at the library for forty-five mins.

And renting their laptops is <u>not</u> a vibe.

MOTHER. Did you like being a camper?

CHARITY. No.

Kids were fighting all the time in Harlem.

You gotta do a lot just to fit in.

From the fit, to the tims, to the speech.

I'm too sensitive.

MOTHER. I know. But so are the kids who fight.

CHARITY. *(Says this quicky and runs.)* Auntie and grandma don't like to talk about their moms.

You never met your grandma.

...

Nashelle sent her college essay draft to my email last night.

Cuz. Well. She talked about her ancestry.

And I swear I had a dream last night.

MOTHER. *(She snaps her fingers.)* Get to the point. Say it.

CHARITY. Okay don't get mad.

This morning while you slept.

I used your Chase card to pay for an African Ancestry test.

(**MOTHER** *jolts for her daughter.*)

AND I ordered from ANCESTRY.COM

AND 23andME.

And-and AH I'm sorry.

I don't know what came over me!/

    (*They are circling each other at a table.*)

MOTHER. /YOU'RE THE REASON I WENT INTO OVERDRAFT. CHARITY! NOT OKAY. WHY ARE YOU SO OBBSESSED WITH THIS?! What is coming over you child?! We drop down in Philly and suddenly/

CHARITY. (*She's at the brink of a panic attack.*) /All I see is me. Running. Running with an elastic band attached around my chest, and I'm stuck to this place. And I'm running, but I know I'm. I'm making no sense. Camp here makes me sad. That's all.

    (**CUFFEE** *enters shaken.* **MOTHER** *and* **CHARITY** *try to pretend they're normal and alright.*)

CUFFEE. Hello.

MOTHER.	**CHARITY.**
Hi Cuffee!	Hi Cuffee!

CUFFEE. Group 3's counselors are going to pick up your kids from their lunch block.

MOTHER. Oh. Alright. Is everything okay?

    (**CUFFEE** *shuts the door and sits.*)

CUFFEE. This was a big day of scrambling for us.

MOTHER. What's wrong?

CUFFEE. John didn't show up for work today.

MOTHER. Yeah, we assumed he wasn't feeling well or...

CUFFEE. No. John is gone.

CHARITY. Gone?

CUFFEE. He makes me so angry.

CHARITY. Gone like you don't know where he is?

CUFFEE. No.

He's on his way to Vermont for a production of Hamlet. He will be playing the role of Second Gravedigger.

(**CHARITY** *and* **MOTHER** *laugh.*)

CHARITY. *(While laughing.)* Who's the first?!

CUFFEE. John isn't a good actor.

MOTHER. I didn't know he was an actor!

I can see it though.

He emotes.

CUFFEE. He must have packed overnight.

Because his belongings are gone.

MOTHER. What are you going to do?

CUFFEE. We have floaters.

Offsite.

For temporary coverage.

Until we can officially re-hire.

MOTHER. Thank you.

CUFFEE. I just think he's such an idiot.

CHARITY. Me too.

CUFFEE. Are you both managing alright today?

MOTHER & CHARITY. Managing.

CUFFEE. You had a lesson, today right?

About the phases of the moon?

There was a full moon last night.

MOTHER. Yes!

It went well.

I gotta say

It doesn't seem like you or John like each other very much.

CUFFEE. Charity, cover your ears.

> (**CHARITY** *does so.* **MOTHER** *double covers her ears.)*

We used to have sex.

MOTHER. Okay.

CUFFEE. I know he didn't tell you that.

MOTHER. No.

CUFFEE. So, you can understand?

MOTHER. Nuff said.

> (**MOTHER** *uncovers* **CHARITY**'s *ears then* **CHARITY** *takes her fingers down.)*

CUFFEE. He did leave something for you both.

Dropped it in my office.

How?

When?

Why?

I have no idea.

> (**CUFFEE** *exits.)*

CHARITY. What did he say?

MOTHER. They used to date.

CHARITY. That makes so much sense.

> (**CUFFEE** *re-enters holding a letter, key, and the box [a large red box].*)

CUFFEE. A letter

A key

And a box.

CHARITY. It's eerie.

CUFFEE. Black person to Black people.

I wouldn't open a box that looks like that.

MOTHER. It looks old.

CHARITY. So old.

CUFFEE. *(Looks at cellphone.)* Hold on, I need to make the announcement.

> (**CUFFEE** *runs to his office.* **MOTHER** *and* **CHARITY** *eat while staring at the box.*)

(Voice over.) Group Three. Please pick-up Group Two from the Lunchroom.

Group 3. Please pick-up Group Two from the Lunchroom.

Happy 4th of July! ...hm. Okay.

> (*Silence. Munching. The food is blehhh today.* **CUFFEE** *re-enters.*)

Are you going to read the letter?

> (**MOTHER** *opens the letter.*)

MOTHER. *(She reads John's writing aloud.)* So much guilt.

(Rolls her eyes.) So many questions.

Not sure why or how

The whispers told me

CUFFEE. *(Sotto voice.)* The whispers?

MOTHER. This belonged to you.

CHARITY. I have a bad feeling.

MOTHER. *(Reads the letter aloud.)* You asked me

(Confused.)

If I felt the "weight of time" last night.

I felt my **responsibility to it**.

I am a coward for not giving it to you myself.

I apologize for it.

CUFFEE. What is going on?

CHARITY. Thank you for bringing this to us.

CUFFEE. Okay...

MOTHER. Thank you.

CUFFEE. Okay.

MOTHER. We're gonna do some freaky shit tonight.

CUFFEE. Where? Here?

MOTHER. Yes.

CUFFEE. Like what kind of/

CHARITY. /The box. We're opening it. Right ma?

*(**MOTHER** nods.)*

CUFFEE. Now?

CHARITY. No, at night, while everyone's asleep.

(**MOTHER** *nods in cool agreement.*)

CUFFEE. Ya'll are sounding funny.

MOTHER. We know.

CUFFEE. You know how you're both sounding right now?

Right?

Real odd.

(**CUFFEE** *exits.* **CHARITY** *and* **MOTHER** *stare at the box, and decide to distract themselves.*)

MOTHER. I've never seen July 4th as my holiday.

CHARITY. Just, Juneteenth.

MOTHER. It felt strange. Hearing Cuffee say that date, so cheerfully. I feel conflicted about it.

(**CHARITY** *rises.*)

CHARITY. Might as well go and pick up the little ones.

MOTHER. Why so soon my daughter?

CHARITY.   Because we just finished our meeting with Cuffee.

MOTHER. …

CHARITY. (*Checking her watch.*) Group 3 goes on lunch in like fifteen minutes.

MOTHER. Sit.

(**CHARITY** *does so.*)

(*Beat.*)

CHARITY. You know what's been on my mind?

MOTHER. Grandma?

CHARITY. Last night, when we got back, grandma kept talking to me about getting into "Africa's Heaven". And I wonder, is there a heaven for each of us on each continent? Or is it more of a Black heaven/Asian heaven/White heaven/Indigenous Heaven? Are we separated?

MOTHER. Not sure.

CHARITY. Aren't we all supposed to be "one" when we get there? Like shouldn't I see a Latine human in heaven?

MOTHER. It depends on what Jesus looks like in the "Jesus photo" you have in your church. Maybe you go to THAT heaven!

CHARITY. There can't be different Jesus'.

MOTHER. WELL MY Jesus is Black.

> *("Beautiful" by Snoop Dogg and Pharrell Williams plays* with the lyrics of the first few seconds...* **CUFFEE** *enters with a suitcase, opens it, and there's multiple amounts of different Jesus costumes.)*

My Jesus wears a red suit.

> *(***CUFFEE** *puts on that suit.)*

CHARITY. With a feather hat and alligator shoes.

> *(***CUFFEE** *does so.)*

Wait. Jesus loves animals. Jesus wouldn't want that.

My Jesus wears Jordans.

> *(***CUFFEE** *does so. He keeps one alligator shoe on and places on one Jordan sneaker.)*

Why do you have Jesus as a man in your mind?

---

* A licence to produce *The Great Privation* does not include a performance licence for any third-party or copyrighted recordings. Licensees should create their own.

MOTHER. I've never had a father figure, so that's why it feels good to think of Jesus in that way.

CHARITY. I feel the same way since Daddy's passing.

My Jesus

He plays basketball.

>   (**CUFFEE** *dribbles a basketball.*)

He knows how to hang.

He can dance.

>   (**CUFFEE** *dances.*)

It's a party.

>   (*Lights shift.*)

Everyone has an Afro.

>   (*A stage manager throws two afros to* **CHARITY** *and one to* **MOTHER**. **CUFFEE** *wears one as well.*)

>   (*They dance.* **CUFFEE** *and* **MOTHER** *do some old school moves.* **CHARITY** *does the latest dance of the Black youth.*)

MOTHER. In my heaven

Jesus has given me my own shack on an island.

>   (**CUFFEE** *hands* **MOTHER** *keys.*)

And we sing all day and praise him.

>   (*A church piano rings through our eyes and a choir of Black people singing "Praise!" erupts in our ears.*)

CHARITY. If we all have different versions of heaven

Does Jesus place us in our own special place?

I feel like we're putting a lot on Jesus.

MOTHER. Maybe.

CHARITY. But I like the idea of African heaven.

It's encouraging for me.

Like maybe we could meet all of our ancestors

Maybe they could tell us what they were like.

Wouldn't that be fun?

MOTHER. I would just hope we can GET along with all our ancestors.

(To African Jesus.) Thank you African Jesus! You can go.

> *(**CUFFEE** exits.)*

CHARITY. As long as we get to see Daddy again!

MOTHER. Yeah.

> *(The tree grows new leaves. Some green. Some red. Some yellow. **MOTHER** and **CHARITY** see it, roam outside to the grave, and touch the leaves. It immediately turns to night on stage.)*

Scene Eight

(The timer shines numbers to signify the year we're in [whatever year the production is taking place]. **MOTHER** *and* **CHARITY** *sit with the box and shovel between them.)*

MOTHER. Baby?

CHARITY. Yes, Mommie.

MOTHER. I feel like I should prepare you.

CHARITY. Okay.

MOTHER. I'm not sure.

I'm confused at the feeling inside of me.

CHARITY. I feel strangely connected.

Not to the box.

But, its contents.

No, need to prepare me.

MOTHER. We've never spoken deeply of the horrors of our country.

CHARITY. We have.

MOTHER. Not of the past.

CHARITY. You've told me things

You have.

MOTHER. So, what do you assume to be in this box?

CHARITY. Bones mama.

MOTHER. You look at the world with this joy.

With this uncontrollable joy.

I was never sure, if you feel the loss in your gut.

CHARITY. Then, it's possible you don't know me well enough.

MOTHER. That's awful to say.

CHARITY. I feel the pain.

Laughing is a small dose of Advil for it.

John passed a burden onto us tonight.

He didn't give us a chance to say no.

MOTHER. Classic white people.

CHARITY. Regardless.

I can't shake the feeling I have.

MOTHER. Do you ever go to different places in New York and feel a sad memory?

Kinda like the one we feel here?

A connection?

CHARITY. Sure.

At museums.

MOTHER. Which ones?

CHARITY. The MET!

I feel sad there.

MOTHER. Really?

CHARITY. I feel a distance.

They have this harsh yellow light on the African artifacts in there.

Unlike any other part of the museum.

It's trying so hard to remind me that I'm in Africa.

The yellow light is trying hard to be Africa's sun.

It heightens the feeling that we're in America with Africa's stuff.

MOTHER. You think it should go back?

CHARITY. Maybe.

I think they need to change their lighting.

And stop having White British people do the audio descriptions for artifacts.

(In a Nigerian dialect.) DI COLONIZERS.

MOTHER. Have you ever felt the kind of connection in New York that you feel here in Philly, now?

CHARITY. Never.

Ever.

MOTHER. I wish we could talk to Grandma about it.

CHARITY. Me too. I wore Auntie down a little down this morning.

She said all our ancestors are from here in Philadelphia.

She's sure about the three generations back.

> *(**MOTHER** brings the box and kneels beside the grave. **CHARITY** follows. They open the box. It's a skull.)*

MOTHER. #5. Moses Freeman.

CHARITY. That's your maiden name.

MOTHER. Yeah. Why is it in Sharpie? It's looks freshly written.

CHARITY. John talked about letters

And notes.

Diaries.

Maybe. Maybe. He put it together.

> *(**CUFFEE** enters.)*

CUFFEE. Sorry I'm late. Nineteen words. Ready?

Your eleven-year-olds-got their hands on a tub of expired cookie dough. And got sixteen campers sick.

> (**MOTHER** *and daughter make an "ouch face".*
> **CUFFEE** *sees the skull.)*

Woah.

A skull.

Freaky for sure.

Whose is it?

CHARITY. Some great.

Great.

Great.

Grandpa? Uncle?

I don't know!

MOTHER. There's a possibility we're going crazy.

CUFFEE. What do you need?

MOTHER. To bury it.

CUFFEE. Did John murder someone?

CHARITY. Worse.

CUFFEE. *(Reading the skull.)* Moses Freeman.

CHARITY. Yeah, Freeman is my mom's maiden name.

CUFFEE. And we're not calling the cops?

CHARITY. Nah.

But, the word on the ancestral streets is – John's ancestors

Fucked our ancestors up.

It's insane.

(**CUFFEE** *gets the shovel and digs.*)

CUFFEE. He's so selfish

Making us bury it back.

CHARITY. So selfish.

MOTHER. So selfish.

We'll see him again.

CHARITY. We'll all jump his ass.

CUFFEE. Glad I'm here to help.

CHARITY.	**MOTHER**.
Thank you.	Thank you.

MOTHER. Your family, are they from here as well?

CUFFEE. Yes, they are.

Very proud of it.

MOTHER. Are you close with them?

CUFFEE. Yes, and no.

My immediate family is here.

My distant relatives want no parts of Philadelphia.

MOTHER. SO you know a little about your ancestry then?

CUFFEE. It's a touchy topic.

I assume I'll find out when my parents are on their deathbeds.

That's typically when you find out the truth.

And finally your life begins to make a little bit more sense.

MOTHER. You think, we carry our ancestors with us?

CUFFEE. No.

I do think there are hints they leave for us though.

In our walk.

Or maybe

I don't know.

In the soil.

I don't know.

AH.

This is weird.

Ya'll this is weird.

But, I've never felt so alive.

CHARITY. *(Gesturing for the shovel.)* We can take it from here. Thank you Cuffee.

>   *(**CUFFEE** walks towards the exit.)*

CUFFEE. You know when I think about my relatives.

From what little I've overheard.

They've always been the first at something.

The first Black person to do this career.

Or have that degree.

Own this fancy car. You name it.

I'm the first Black **and** Queer program supervisor at this white ass camp.

What I think I've learned so far in this position this summer; being the first can make you cold.

Brainwashed. Private.

It's like – I'm proud – I'm proud of myself too.

Because it takes a lot to get where I've gotten.

It takes passion.

When I look at you both, I see people who are sure about their feelings and instincts.

I can only hope, to be so in touch one day.

...

Look out for an announcement at dawn, I'll confirm if we all still have jobs or not. It will depend on if these campers don't die in their sleep from salmonella.

You know where to reach me.

> *(**CUFFEE** exits. **CHARITY** digs.)*

CHARITY. *(Singing.)*
 I'M DIGGIN'
 I'M DIGGIN'
 O
 I'M DIGGIN'
 I'M DIGGIN'
 O

MOTHER.	CHARITY.
Please. Stop.	I'M DIGGIN'

CHARITY.
 SO DEEOOOP O
 CAINT SLEEP

MOTHER. Charity

CHARITY.
 CAINT SLEEP
 O
 DIS HEAT.
 DIS HEAT.
 O

MOTHER. Charity, shut up!

CHARITY. I feel like I need to sing a Negro Spiritual.

MOTHER. What chu know about some Negro Spiritual girl?

CHARITY. I know! I've done my research!

MOTHER. I'm pretty sure Moses gon' come after you.

He'll haunt your dreams with that mess you be tellin'.

You can't be activatin' spirits and whatnot.

Making em' mad.

CHARITY. *(Rapping.)*
BACK IT UP
BACK IT UP
THROW IT BACK
LIKE A TRUCK
MY KITTY BIG
ASS UP.

MOTHER. Charity.

That's not good for the planet.

Your rappin' is the new pollution.

CHARITY. *(Rapping.)*
THROW IT BACK
THROW IT BACK.
LIKE A TRUCK
LIKE A TRUCK
MY KITTY BIG
ASS UP.

MOTHER. Don't make me pop you.

CHARITY. Fine.

(**CHARITY** *hits a box.*)

Woah.

(**CHARITY** *jumps in the grave.*)

MOTHER. BE careful.

> (**CHARITY** *opens the box.*)

CHARITY. This grave was broken into.

There's a carving on the top.

It says Moses Freeman.

This is freaky mom.

> (**MOTHER** *hands* **CHARITY** *the skull.*)

MOTHER. Should I take a picture for auntie and grandma?

CHARITY. No mom. They might have heart attacks.

(Placing Moses' skull in the casket.) Moses Freeman.

You get your rest now.

Okay?

> (**CHARITY** *hops out of the grave. She sits in
> a way, that her arms hang over the grave.
> She groups some of the soil in her hands.
> She prays.* **MOTHER** *joins on the opposite
> side, grabs the soil, and prays. A moment of
> silence.*)

MOTHER. Why do I still feel weight?

CHARITY. *(Surprised by the words coming out of her
mouth.)* Jesus, I'm hoping to die when it's warm. They
don't come when it's warm. *(Needing her* **MOTHER**.*)* An
ugly past is pounding on my brain. Over and Over.

MOTHER. Come here.

CHARITY. I hate that I don't feel better.

I feel angry.

This is my past?

Is this what I'm left with to know about our lineage?

Violence is my tethering?

I-I.

I feel like/

MOTHER. /It's unfair.

It's so so unfair.

CHARITY. How can you bear it?

I still feel the pain inside of me.

These bones haunt me mama.

Aren't they everywhere?

How can you bear to walk outside anymore?

MOTHER. I could give you my answer.

But, as you continue growin' older in this country.

Your answer will be different from mine.

Every Black person has their own answer.

The pain and anger and grief turning inside me

Sometimes I let it sit so my ancestors never feel alone.

New pains come through though.

As the past that we are promised no longer exists repeats and invades our present disguised as something new.

I've learned to let the movement inside.

That pain.

Help me dance harder.

I go with it.

> (*A sunrise. They embrace.* **MOTHER** *hands* **DAUGHTER** *her phone back.*)

Here.

You want to know something?

I re-shared your Tiktok.

I posted, "This is Minnie Chillous, Charity's mama re-sharing this".

So, the school can come after me not you.

I'm on your side.

…

I see the shabooya chant is trending like it's something new.

You know that stuff has been around for ages?

CHARITY. I'll shabooya with you mama.

Don't get too excited.

But, it's like, keep your rizz up.

I can't be lookin' wack on that app.

My friends will drag me.

> (**CHARITY** *hands her phone to an audience member.*)

Help us out will you?

(The phone.) Keep it vertical.

> (*A Dreamgirls-like finale lighting interrupts the moment. The TikTok sound [counting a recording in] plays.*)

MOTHER.
SHABOOYA SHA SHA
SHA BOOYA ROLL
CALL
MY NAME IS MINNIE   **CHARITY**.
                                          Yeah?!

AND I AM FINE
>   Yeah?!

AND WHEN I SHAKE
IT?
>   Yeah?!

THEY BE LIKE SHE
DIVINE.
ROLLCALL

>   (**CUFFEE** *appears from the audience.*)

CUFFEE.   *(Queer man joy.)* Ya'll SHABOOYA-IN'?
AHHHH!!!

CHARITY.
SHABOOYA SHA SHA
SHA BOOYA ROLL
CALL
MY NAME IS CHARITY **MOTHER & CUFFEE**.
>   Yeah?!

I'm From New York.
>   Yeah?!

I don't eat pork.

>   (**CHARITY**'s *a little off beat, but* **MOM** *and*
>   **CUFFEE** *ain't gon' judge her too hard*)

>   Yeah????

But when I eat it.
DEY say UH COURSE.
ROLLCALL

>   (**CHARITY** *did too much with her Shabooya,*
>   *but* **MOTHER** *and* **CUFFEE** *want to support her.*)

>   **MOTHER & CUFFEE**.
>   Yeah...

CUFFEE.
>SHABOOYA SHA SHA
>SHA BOOYA ROLL
>CALL
>MY NAME IS CUFFEE.

MOTHER & CHARITY.
>YEAH.

I like to dance.

>YEAH.

And when I shake it

>Yeah!

They say DAYUM.
ROLL CALL.

MOTHER, CUFFEE & CHARITY.
>ROLL CALL.

>*(They snap, they shaybooya a couple of more times and decrease in volume. They laugh and hug.)*

MOTHER. *(To the audience.)* Hi everyone.

We love you.

All of us is all of us, and aren't we all here today?

That's by Gilbert M. Fletcher.

But, I'd like to end us on an Alice Walker Quote

Are you ready?

"To remember is to plan"

Let the music play.

>*(Followed by Dope Saint Jude's "Go High Go Low".*)*

>*(Followed by C-Muder, Majic, and Snoop Dogg's "Down For My Niggaz".*)*

(Followed by Melinda Doolittle "Lift Every Voice And Sing".*)

(I'd like, upon audience members readying themselves to leave the theater's building, in the lobby, there to be a long vertical banner that hangs in the theater space, which can be written on by attendees. **"Bodies are still subject to being used for Medical Research without consent** *from that person.* Especially folk who are a part of an unhoused population. It varies from state to state but the research is alarming."*)*

End of Play

GIFT

If you are Black, this is for you. If you are not Black, discard.
I want to thank you for sitting through this play. Some of you may know
every single ancestor you've ever had. Some of you may not. I want you
to know, I am a Black woman from Harlem, and I know it can be quite
a bit to sit through a play about a history we cannot change.

If you have thoughts "good, bad, or indifferent" that you'd like me to
know, I will take them gratefully, and I want you to know that if you
send thoughts my way, I will place what you say *not including your
name*" on my website. This will remain on a private page, which only
"US" *Black fist* can access.

PLEASE SEND THOUGHTS TO: niaakilahrobinson@gmail.com
If you'd like to see how other Black folk feel about my play or your
comment posted... It'll be on my website...www.niaakilahrobinson.com
Please click: TGP
Password: TGPBLACK
(*I might also have a scene hidden there that didn't make it into the play!*)

But if you don't have the time or a desire to.

I walk by this mirror on 135th street between Frederick Douglass Ave
and Adam Clayton Powell Jr. Blvd quite often. Whoever placed it, knew
us Harlem residents needed a reminder, and I wanted to pass on a
small part of my home to you.

"YOUR LIFE MATTERS"

DICTIONARY

Wapper: *noun* A fish; a name given to the smaller species of the river gudgeon.